Table of Contents

To the Student

In the United States, government is based on the consent of those governed. Ideally, this consent is given by a caring and informed public. *Government by Consent II* provides information about United States and Texas government and politics to help you understand how government affects your life. As you better understand the workings of government and how it affects your life, you will become more involved in the process. The more involved you become; the more effect you will have on the system.

This course examines the United States Congress and the Texas Legislature. It examines the legislative process and its relationship to the Presidency. The Chief Executives and bureaucracies from the perspective of the national government and from the position of the states are explored. The national and state judiciary, the judicial process, and individual rights are described. Each lesson is designed to make you a better informed citizen, more capable of consenting to government through rational choice.

The two primary purposes of *Government by Consent II* are to provide you with the knowledge to make informed decisions about United States and Texas government and politics, and to help you understand that **you,** as an individual, **can** make a difference in what government does. In 1963 Martin Luther King Jr. wrote a remarkable "Letter from Birmingham City Jail." It is reprinted following Lesson 25 because it gives you a first-person account of how one person applied his knowledge of American government in a way that still affects millions of people today. The combination of television and textbook, directed by this Study Guide, will help you understand how government works, but, more importantly, that **you** can make a difference in what your government does.

Course Organization

Government by Consent II is designed as a comprehensive learning system consisting of three elements: Study Guide, textbook, and telelessons.

Study Guide
This Study Guide acts as your daily instructor. For each lesson it gives you an overview, learning objectives, textbook reading assignment, focus points, key terms for both textbook and telelesson, recommended readings, projects for becoming more involved in the political process, and a self test. If you

follow the Study Guide recommendations and view each lesson carefully, you should successfully accomplish all of the requirements for this course.

Textbook

Schmidt, Steffen W., Mack C. Shelley II, and Barbara A. Bardes. *American Government and Politics Today*, 1993-94 edition. St. Paul, Minnesota: West Publishing Company, 1993.

Jones, Eugene, *et al. Practicing Texas Politics*, 8th edition. Dallas, Texas: Houghton Mifflin Company, 1992.

or

Jones, Eugene, *et al. Practicing Texas Politics – A Brief Survey*, 4th edition. Dallas, Texas: Houghton Mifflin Company, 1993.

You are responsible for only **one** of the two *Practicing Texas Politics* textbooks. It is your resonsibility to know which book is used in your class.

Each textbook provides essential and interesting information about the government and politics of this nation. In the Schmidt book, key terms are defined in side margins. In the Jones books, key terms are defined either in the body of the chapter or in the glossary. Specific reading assignments for each lesson appear in the Study Guide, just prior to the Textbook Focus Points. Be certain to read the assignment **before** viewing the lesson.

Telelessons
Each telelesson is correlated to a specific reading assignment. The better prepared you are before you view the lesson, the more you will learn. It is imperative that you read and understand your assignment and study the key terms before viewing the telelesson. The telelessons are packed with information, so watch them closely. If the lessons are broadcast more than once in your area, or if video or audio tapes are available at your college, you might find it helpful to watch the telelessons again or listen to audio tapes for review. Since examination questions will be taken from the telelessons as well as from the textbook, careful attention to both is vital to your success.

Study Guidelines

The quickest and most efficient way for you to cover the important points in each lesson is to follow these study guidelines. For every lesson:

1. Read the **Overview, Learning Objectives, Key Terms** and **Textbook Focus Points** for the lesson.

2. Complete the **Textbook Reading Assignment**, keeping the **Key Terms** and **Textbook Focus Points** in mind.

3. Write your responses to the **Textbook Focus Points**, going back to the text if you aren't certain you know the answers.

4. Read the names of the major **Telelesson Interviewees**, then examine the **Telelesson Focus Points**.

5. View the telelesson with the **Key Terms** and **Telelesson Focus Points** in mind. Take only brief notes while viewing.

6. Immediately after viewing the telelesson, write detailed responses to the **Telelesson Focus Points**, referring to your notes to help you.

7. Define each **Key Term**.

8. Take the **Self Test** to check your understanding of the concepts presented in the lesson.

9. Compare your answers to the **Answer Key** located at the end of the lesson. If you answered incorrectly, the key provides references so that you can review the material from which each question was taken.

10. Extend your learning by studying some of the **Recommended Readings** and acting on one or more of the suggestions for **Getting Involved**.

Lesson 1

Congress

Overview

Article I of the Constitution describes and lists the powers of the legislative branch of government: Congress. This lesson shows how the two houses are organized and who the leaders are. It also covers the committee system, in preparation for the next lesson on the legislative process.

At times in the history of the U.S. Congress, all of the power was held by a few senior members in leadership positions: the speaker of the House, the Senate majority leader, and the chairs of the standing committees. These few individuals decided the fate of most bills. But the reforms of the 1970s diffused congressional power. These reforms brought about needed changes, but they also created major stumbling blocks for legislation.

Another problem Congress faces is a negative public opinion of what it does—and doesn't—do. This is based in part on the small percentage of bills that it passes and a belief that Congress focuses on its own self interest and not on the interests of its constituents. An important part of this lesson addresses the public's role in the legislative process and examines how members of Congress gather information and opinions about pending legislation. If you and others like you are not participating in the legislative process, who is filling that void?

To better appreciate what members of Congress do, the television portion of the lesson follows a representative and a senator through the hectic schedule of a normal day. The intent of this lesson is to examine Congress and its operation, and to emphasize the responsibility that we all share for what Congress does and does not accomplish.

Learning Objectives

Goal: The purpose of "Congress" is to review the organization and structure of the House and Senate and to illustrate how representatives and senators integrate their own needs and those of their constituencies into their elected roles.

Objectives:

1. Explain the rationale for a bicameral Congress, cite the primary functions of Congress, and contrast the major similarities and differences between the House and the Senate.

2. Define and give examples of the "enumerated," or expressed, powers of Congress.

3. Outline two theories of representation to justify whether Congress is or is not truly a "constituent care" organization.

4. Describe the ethics questions facing Congress today, especially in the context of how the question of ethics may affect members' decisions about voting and handling "perks" and other privileges.

5 Explain the committee structure and formal leadership of the House and of the Senate.

6. Briefly describe what is required in order to prepare the national budget, and explain why the process is so complex.

7. Contrast the diffusion of power in Congress now with the way it was prior to the early 1970s, especially as this affects congressional operations.

8. Summarize the activities in a typical day in Washington, D.C., for a senator or representative, and note how these activities affect you.

Key Terms

Watch for these terms and pay particular attention to what each one means, as you follow the textbook and telelesson.

Bicameralism
Enumerated powers
"Necessary and proper"
  ("elastic") clause
Lawmaking
Trustees
Instructed delegates
Oversight
Rules committee
Filibustering
Cloture
Franking
Standing committee

Select committee
Joint committee
Conference committees
Seniority system
Safe seat
Speaker of the House
Majority Leader of the House
House Minority leader
Whips
President *pro tempore*
Senate majority floor leader
Senate minority floor leader

Textbook Reading Assignment

Schmidt, Shelley, and Bardes. *American Government and Politics Today*, 1993-94 edition. Chapter 12, "The Congress," pp. 377-390, 398-410, 414-421.

Textbook Focus Points

Before you read the textbook assignment, review the following points to help focus your thoughts. After you complete the assignment, write out your responses to reinforce what you have learned.

1. Why does the United States have a bicameral Congress?

2. What are "enumerated," or expressed, powers? List some of the enumerated powers of Congress.

3. What are the primary functions of Congress?

4. What are two theories of representation?

5. What are the major differences between the House and the Senate in terms of size, length of term, organization, and operation?

6. How can you decide if members of Congress truly represent you?

7. What are some of the perquisites ("perks") and other privileges of being a member of Congress?

8. How are the committees structured in the House and in the Senate?

9. What is the formal leadership of the House and the Senate?

10. How do members of Congress decide how to vote?

11. What all is involved in preparing the national budget?

12. How does the question of ethics affect Congress today?

Telelesson Interviewees

The following individuals share their expertise in the telelesson:

Thomas S. Foley–Democrat; U.S. Representative, State of Washington; Speaker of the House

Barbara Jordan–Professor, LBJ School of Public Affairs, University of Texas, Austin

Charles Percy–Republican; Former U.S. Senator, Illinois

Patricia Saiki–Republican; U.S. Representative, Hawaii

Mike Synar–Democrat; U.S. Representative, Oklahoma

Telelesson Focus Points

Before you view the telelesson, read over the following points to help focus your thoughts. After the presentation, write out your responses to help you remember these important points.

1. Who had real power in Congress before the early 1970s, and how was that power obtained?

2. How did the committee reforms of the 1970s diffuse, or spread, power in the House and in the Senate among more people?

3. How does this new diffusion of power affect the operation of Congress?

4. Is Congress a "constituent care" organization? How does this affect the relationship between the members of Congress and their constituents?

5. What is a typical day like in the life of a senator and a representative, and what parts of it benefit you?

Recommended Reading

The following suggestions are not required reading except when assigned by your instructor. They are listed to let you know where you can find additional information on areas which interest you.

Broder, David. "Who Took the Fun Out of Congress?" *The Washington Post Weekly Edition* (February 17, 1986).

Champagne, Anthony. *Congressman Sam Rayburn*. New Brunswick, N.J.: Rutgers University Press, 1984.

Miller, William M. *Fishbait: The Memoirs of the Congressional Doorkeeper*. Englewood Cliffs, N.J.: Prentice-Hall, 1977.

"The World of Congress." *Newsweek* (April 24, 1989): pp. 28-34.

Getting Involved

These activities are not required unless your instructor assigns them. But they offer good suggestions to help you understand and become more involved in the political process.

1. Note the "Getting Involved" section in your textbook at the end of Chapter 12.

2. Most members of Congress, especially House members, hold "town hall" meetings several times a year. Attend one to see how many constituents participate and what kind of questions they ask. Also note how the member of Congress uses staff members to handle constituent concerns.

Self Test

After reading the assignment and watching the telelesson, you should be able to answer these questions. When you have completed the test, turn to the Answer Key to score your answers.

1. Trying to balance the big states' population advantage and the small states' demand for equality, the founders created through the U.S. Constitution a(n)
   a. unicameral legislature.
   b. bicameral legislature.
   c. elite class.
   d. legislative assembly.

2. The enumerated powers of Congress are powers
   a. written into the U.S. Constitution.
   b. that Congress has given itself by passing laws.
   c. created by decisions of the Supreme Court.
   d. that are vague and often disputed by strong presidents.

3. Most constituents expect individual members of Congress to
   a. support legislation that is in the best interest of the country, regardless of its impact on their constituents.
   b. support the ideas of the member's political party.
   c. support the major ideas of the president.
   d. act as a broker between the needs of private citizens and the requirements of the federal government.

4. The two theories of representation are
   a. trustee and individualism.
   b. trustee and instructed delegate.
   c. individualism and instructed delegate.
   d. trustee and ombudsman.

5. One major difference between the House and the Senate is the number of members in each, which means that the
    a. House will spend more time than the Senate debating a bill on the floor.
    b. Senate can act on a bill more quickly than the House.
    c. House needs more rules.
    d. Senate is less experienced in debate.

6. Many members of the U.S. Senate and House of Representatives are not typical American citizens, because they are
    a. older and have more political experience than most Americans.
    b. younger than most Americans.
    c. more religious and less educated.
    d. nonwhite and female.

7. Members of Congress are granted generous franking privileges that
    a. permit them to mail letters without charge to their constituents.
    b. allow them to charge items to a special expense account.
    c. allow them unlimited calls to their district without charge.
    d. give them four round-trip air fares to their district each year.

8. Which one of the following does the committee structure NOT accomplish?
    a. It allows members to concentrate on a limited number of subjects.
    b. It restricts members' opportunity to give input.
    c. It provides for a division of labor in the legislature.
    d. It allows members to develop expertise in drafting legislation.

9. The formal leadership organization of Congress
   a. is strictly provided for in the Constitution.
   b. depends on the president.
   c. is based on political parties.
   d. has changed very little since the first Congress in 1789.

10. Most people who study the decision-making process in Congress agree that one of the best predictors for how a member will vote is his or her
    a. party membership.
    b. affiliation with organized interest groups.
    c. length of time in Congress.
    d. age and length of tenure.

11. The national budget is prepared by
    a. the president and the president's staff, then presented to Congress.
    b. the Senate majority leader, then presented to Congress.
    c. a bureaucratic agency, then presented to Congress.
    d. bureaucratic agencies, the president and presidential staff, and both chambers of Congress.

12. The most serious public-relations problem confronting Congress is
    a. its inability to defeat the president's legislative program.
    b. citizen concern about congressional ethics.
    c. the massive salary increases in the past four years.
    d. the lack of use of the War Powers Act during major foreign-policy disputes with the president.

13. For years, much of the power in Congress rested in
    a. select committees.
    b. conference committees.
    c. standing committees.
    d. interim committees.

14. The committee reforms of the 1970s broke the South's stranglehold on committee chairs by shifting the power from
    a. select committees to conference committees.
    b. senior committee members to freshman members.
    c. standing committees to subcommittees.
    d. conference committees to joint committees.

15. This new diffusion of power in Congress has
    a. added new layers of legislative interests.
    b. reduced the power of the president of the Senate.
    c. increased the pressure on the president.
    d. brought more cases to the Supreme Court.

16. Because members of Congress are concerned about being re-elected, which one of the following do they NOT try to do to keep their constituencies happy?
    a. Solve simple but visible problems for constituents
    b. Give the appearance of being responsible
    c. Accept large donations from rival organizations so as to hurt no one's feelings
    d. Return to their districts often to maintain close personal contact

Short-Answer Questions:
17. Give an overview of a typical day in the life of a senator or representative, and tell whether these actions reflect what you think a member of Congress ought to be doing.

18. Summarize what you see as the weaknesses of the House and the Senate.

19. Summarize what you see as the strengths of the House and the Senate.

Answer Key

These are the correct answers with reference to the Learning Objectives, and to the source of the information: the Textbook Focus Points, Schmidt, *et al. American Government and Politics Today* (Schmidt), and the Telelesson Focus Points. Page numbers are also given for the Textbook Focus Points. "KT" indicates questions with Key Terms defined.

Question	Answer	Learning Objective	Textbook Focus Point (page no.)	Telelesson Focus Point
1	B	1	1 (Schmidt, p. 380)............KT	
2	A	2	2 (Schmidt, p. 380)............KT	
3	D	1	3 (Schmidt, p. 382)	
4	B	3	4 (Schmidt, p. 383)............KT	
5	C	1	5 (Schmidt, p. 385)	
6	A	3	6 (Schmidt, p. 388)	4
7	A	4	7 (Schmidt, p. 399)............KT	
8	B	5	8 (Schmidt, p. 401)	3
9	C	5	9 (Schmidt, p. 405)	
10	A	4	10 (Schmidt, p. 410)	3
11	D	6	11 (Schmidt, p. 414)	
12	B	4	12 (Schmidt, p. 416)	
13	C	7	8 (Schmidt, p. 402)............KT	1
14	C	7		2
15	A	7		3
16	C	3		4

Short Answers:

17		8		5
18		1	5 (Schmidt, pp. 380-388)	2
19		1	5 (Schmidt, pp. 380-388)	2

Lesson 2

The Texas Legislature

Overview

Of the three branches of Texas government—executive, legislative and judicial—the legislative branch is the most powerful. Like other legislative bodies, the Texas legislature makes law and public policy. But it also redistricts itself as well as all Texas seats in the U.S. House of Representatives; performs judicial, electoral, administrative, investigatory, and constituent functions; and controls the bureaucracy through the sunset and budget processes.

Yet the 150 members of the Texas House of Representatives and thirty-one members of the Texas Senate meet in regular session for only 140 days every odd-numbered year. This idea of limiting legislative sessions grew out a nineteenth-century idea that legislative service is only a part-time job.

However, in the latter part of the twentieth century, the legislature has been called into special session numerous times. In addition, members serve on committees between regular sessions and address needs of their constituents throughout the year. Today, legislative service is becoming a full-time career.

The lesson defines the size and role of the Texas legislature and discusses the importance of the redistricting process. It also examines the leadership of the House and Senate by illustrating the control over the legislative process exercised by the Speaker of the Texas House of Representatives and the Lieutenant Governor.

Lobbyists are individuals who attempt to influence the outcome of public policy by attempting to persuade (lobby) legislators to reflect the lobbyists' point of view. Lobbyists may represent an interest group or corporation or simply be concerned individuals who believe strongly in an issue. Pamela Fredrich, Director of Common Cause of Texas, and Don Adams, an attorney and lobbyist, outline the part lobbyists play in the legislative process. David Clinkscale of Tarrant County Junior College gives his opinion of the proper role of lobbyists in the legislature.

Learning Objectives

Goal: The purpose of this lesson is to is to describe the composition, organization, and structure of the Texas Senate and House of Representatives as they relate to policy making in Texas.

Objectives:

1. Describe the influence of state legislators and lobbyists on policy making in Texas.

2. Recall factual information associated with serving in the Texas legislature: term of office, types and length of sessions, salary, expense allowances, and qualifications.

3. Discuss the process used in Texas to establish the size and boundaries of the state House of Representatives, the state Senate, and the U.S. House of Representatives.

4. Explain the working structure of the Texas legislature, including the duties and powers of presiding officers and the formation and leadership of standing committees.

Key Terms

Watch for these terms and pay particular attention to what each one means, as you follow the textbook and telelesson.

Bicameral	*Reynolds v Sims*
Regular session	*Kilgarlin v Martin*
Special session	**Per diem allowance**
Redistricting	**Impeachment**

Textbook Reading Assignment

Jones, Ericson, Brown, and Trotter. *Practicing Texas Politics,* 8th edition. Chapter 6, "The Legislature," pp. 242-297, especially pp. 242-268 and 281-297.

Jones, Ericson, Brown, Trotter, and Lynch. *Practicing Texas Politics – A Brief Survey*, 4th edition. Chapter 6, "The Legislature," pp. 148-188, especially pp. 148-170 and 182-188.

Note to students: You are responsible for only *one* of the books listed above. It is your responsibility to know which book is used in your class.

Textbook Focus Points

Before you read the textbook assignment, review the following points to help focus your thoughts. After you complete the assignment, write out your responses to reinforce what you have learned.

1. How does the Texas legislature participate in policy making?

2. What are the terms of office for members of the Texas House and Senate? What are the differences between a regular session of the Texas legislature and a called special session?

3. Explain the process of redistricting.

4. What is the salary of a member of the Texas legislature? What is the expense allowance of members of the legislature when the legislature is in regular or called special session?

5. What are the constitutional qualifications and informal characteristics for serving in the Texas legislature?

6. Describe the duties and powers of the presiding officers of the Texas House and Senate.

7. How are standing committees formed in the Texas legislature? How are chairpersons of standing committees selected?

Telelesson Interviewees

The following individuals will share their expertise in the telelesson:

Don Adams–Attorney and Lobbyist
Ben Barnes–Former Speaker of the Texas House of Representatives; Former Lieutenant Governor of Texas
David Clinkscale–Professor of Government, Tarrant County Junior College
Wilhelmina Delco–Member, Texas House of Representatives, Austin
Pam Fredrich–Director, Common Cause of Texas
Alvin Granoff–Member, Texas House of Representatives, Dallas
William P. Hobby, Jr.–Former Lieutenant Governor of Texas
Gib Lewis–Former Speaker of the Texas House of Representatives
Kaye Northcott–Journalist, *Fort Worth Star Telegram*

Telelesson Focus Points

Before viewing the telelesson, read the following points to help focus your thoughts. After the presentation, write your responses to help you remember these important points.

1. How and by whom are the size and boundaries of the state House of Representatives, state Senate, and U.S. House of Representatives districts determined?

2. According to Gib Lewis and Bill Hobby, what are the most important powers of the presiding officers of the Texas legislature?

3. What is the strongest constitutional and statutory office in Texas?

4. What is the role of lobbyists in the legislative process? What is a lobbyist's most valuable resource? Are lobbyists ethical? What do legislators expect from lobbyists?

Recommended Reading

The following suggestions are not required unless your instructor assigns them. They are listed to let you know where you can find additional information on areas which interest you.

Banks, Jimmy. *Gavels, Grits, and Glory: The Billy Clayton Story*. Burnet, Tx.: Eakin Publications, 1982.
Heard, Robert. *The Miracle of the Killer Bees: 12 Senators Who Changed Texas Politics*. Austin: Honey Hill Publishing Co., 1981.

How the Texas Legislature Works. Dallas: Texas Women's Commission Foundation, 1987.

Texas Monthly Staff. "The Ten Best and the Ten Worst Legislators." *Texas Monthly* (a biennial feature in the July issue following each regular session).

Getting Involved

This activity is not required unless your instructor assigns it. But it offers good suggestions to help you understand and become more involved in the political process.

Discover the names and addresses of your state representative and state senator. If the legislature is in session, write or visit them about an issue of concern to you.

Self Test

After reading the assignment and watching the telelesson, you should be able to answer these questions. When you have completed the test, turn to the Answer Key to score your answers.

1. Passing bills and adopting resolutions are the principal means whereby members of the Texas legislature participate in
   a. action research.
   b. public policy.
   c. strategic planning.
   d. limited bureaucracy.

2. According to the Texas Constitution, the maximum number of special sessions permitted in a single year is
   a. one.
   b. two.
   c. three.
   d. unlimited.

3. Regular sessions of the Texas legislature last
   a. up to 140 days beginning in January of each odd-numbered year.
   b. no more than 140 days each year.
   c. six months (January through June) each year.
   d. year round, without limit on the number of days.

4. Legislative redistricting in Texas takes place every
   a. regular session.
   b. other legislative session.
   c. five years.
   d. ten years.

5. In *Reynolds v Sims* the U. S. Supreme Court held that
   a. both houses of a state legislature must be apportioned on the basis of population.
   b. only one house of a state legislature must be apportioned on the basis of population.
   c. unicameral legislatures are unconstitutional.
   d. legislative districts for state offices could be divided in any manner, so long as that division does not discriminate.

6. Which of the following statements about redistricting in Texas is *not* correct?
   a. The state constitution mandates redistricting after the decennial census.
   b. The Legislative Redistricting Board writes a redistricting plan when the Legislature fails to act.
   c. Redistricting is a nonpolitical process.
   d. Redistricting in Texas is influenced by federal court decisions.

7. Members of the Texas legislature receive a salary of
   a. $7200 per year.
   b. $10,000 per year.
   c. $15,500 per year.
   d. $30,000 per year.

8. Legislative salaries are set by the
   a. Texas Constitution.
   b. Legislative Budget Board.
   c. governor.
   d. plural executive.

9. In terms of percentages, which of the following groups has gained the most representation in the Legislature in the last twenty years?
   a. African-Americans
   b. Hispanics
   c. Male Anglos
   d. Farmers

10. To be a member of the Texas House of Representatives, an individual must have lived in his or her district for
    a. one year.
    b. two years.
    c. five years.
    d. seven years.

11. Constitutional qualifications for Texas state senators and representatives differ with regard to
    a. U.S. citizenship.
    b. age.
    c. voter qualifications.
    d. length of residence in their district.

12. The most important function of the lieutenant governor is to serve as the
    a. secretary of the Senate.
    b. president of the Senate.
    c. president pro tempore of the House.
    d. permanent speaker of the House.

13. Under the terms of the Texas Constitution, the speaker of the House is elected by the
    a. majority party caucus.
    b. registered voters in a general election.
    c. members of the House.
    d. chairs of the House substantive committees.

14. In the Texas House of Representatives, committee chairpersons are appointed by the
    a. senior members of the House.
    b. lieutenant governor.
    c. governor.
    d. speaker of the House.

15. The population of each Texas House district is set by
    a. the Legislative Redistricting Board.
    b. the U.S. Bureau of the Census.
    c. dividing the official census count of Texas by 150.
    d. dividing the interim census count of Texas by 31.

16. According to Gib Lewis and Bill Hobby, the most significant power of a presiding officer of the Texas legislature is the right to
    a. recognize members who wish to speak before the legislature.
    b. vote in order to break a tie.
    c. serve on the Legislative Redistricting Board.
    d. appoint members to standing committees.

17. The most powerful constitutional and statutory office in Texas government is that of the
    a. lieutenant governor.
    b. speaker of the House of Representatives.
    c. comptroller of public accounts.
    d. governor.

18. Lobbyists' most valuable resource is
    a. money.
    b. accurate information.
    c. votes they control.
    d. time.

19. Legislators expect lobbyists to
    a. work for their re-election.
    b. contribute to election campaigns.
    c. explain how legislation affects constituents.
    d. treat them to meals when the legislature is in session.

Short-Answer Question:
  20. Briefly describe the political struggles and judicial actions that highlighted the redistricting conflicts in 1991.

Answer Key

These are the correct answers with reference to the Learning Objectives, and to the source of the information: the Textbook Focus Points, Jones, *et al. Practicing Texas Politics* (Jones) or Jones, *et. al., Practicing Texas Politics — A Brief Survey* (Survey); the Study Guide Overview (Overview); and the Telelesson Focus Points. Page numbers are also given for the Textbook Focus Points. "KT" indicates questions with Key Terms defined.

Question	Answer	Learning Objective	Textbook Focus Point (page no.)	Telelesson Focus Point
1	B	1	1 (Jones, p. 243; Survey, p. 149)	
2	D	2	2 (Jones, p. 245; Survey, pp. 150-151)	
3	A	2	2 (Jones, p. 245; Survey, pp. 150-151)	
4	D	3	3 (Jones, p. 246; Survey, p. 151)	
5	A	3	3 (Jones, p. 246; Survey, p. 151)	
6	C	3	3 (Jones, p. 246; Survey, p. 152)	
7	A	2	4 (Jones, pp. 247-248; Survey, pp. 152-153)	
8	A	2	4 (Jones, p. 248; Survey, p. 152)	
9	A	2	5 (Jones, pp. 250-251; Survey, p. 154)	
10	A	2	5 (Jones, p. 249; Survey, p. 153)	
11	B	2	5 (Jones, p. 249; Survey, pp. 153-154)	
12	B	4	6 (Jones, p. 260; Survey, p. 161)	
13	C	4	6 (Jones, p. 261; Survey, p. 162)	
14	D	4	6 (Jones, pp. 261-262; Survey, pp. 162-163)	
15	C	3		1
16	D	4		2
17	A	4		3
18	B	1		4
19	C	1		4

Short Answer:

20		3	1 (Jones, pp. 285-292; Survey, pp. 182-185)	

Lesson 3

The Legislative Process

Overview

A previous lesson examined the structure and leadership of the U.S. Congress. Here we investigate the legislative process itself.

This lesson gives you a chance to see Congress at work making new laws. It shows you how a bill becomes law by following two specific bills—the Civil Rights Act of 1991 and the Civil Liberties Act (better known as the Japanese Internment and Reparations Bill)—through the stages that a bill must go to become law.

Congress frequently is criticized for the low percentage of bills it passes. But Congress was designed to be a deliberative body, which makes a long road for a bill to travel from when it is first introduced in Congress to when it finally crosses the president's desk. People often point to the relatively small number of bills that eventually do become law as a sign that Congress doesn't accomplish much. But this low number also could indicate that Congress is closely scrutinizing bills and rejecting those that might not be in the best interests of the United States.

One of the major points this lesson makes is that people can influence the legislative process—either as individuals or as groups. The results may not be immediate; as we will see, it took Japanese-Americans interned during World War II over forty years to achieve any results. Yet without public involvement, there are many things Congress might never accomplish—or certainly not in the way we would want. Consequently, this lesson is designed to help you participate effectively in the legislative process, by pointing out the places along the legislative path where your input certainly can make a difference.

Learning Objectives

Goal: The purpose of "The Legislative Process" is to outline basic steps in lawmaking and describe the major factors that influence this process.

Objectives:

1. Describe the fate of a bill when the House and Senate pass different versions, when the president vetoes the bill, and when Congress overrides a presidential veto.

2. Illustrate the legislative process, using the Civil Rights Act of 1991 as an example.

3. State who can draft a bill and who can introduce it, and describe the basic steps a bill goes through to become a law.

4. Tell when and how an individual can affect the legislative process.

5. Explain the reasons why so few bills become law, including strategies that Congress and the president use to delay or stop passage of a bill.

Key Terms

Watch for these terms and pay particular attention to what each one means, as you follow the textbook and telelesson.

Subcommittee(TV)	**Quorum call (TV)**
Rules Committee(TV)	**Veto (TV)**
Conference committee(TV)	**"Pocket veto" (TV)**
Filibuster (TV)	**Override (TV)**

Textbook Reading Assignment

Schmidt, Shelley, and Bardes. *American Government and Politics Today,* 1993-94 edition. Chapter 12, "The Congress," pp. 410-414.

Textbook Focus Points

Before you read the textbook assignment, review the following points to help focus your thoughts. After you complete the assignment, write out your responses to reinforce what you have learned.

1. What happens when the House and Senate pass different versions of the same bill?

2. How may Congress override a presidential veto?

3. What happens to a bill if Congress overrides a presidential veto?

4. What does the passage of the Civil Rights Act of 1991 illustrate about the legislative process?

Telelesson Interviewees

The following individuals share their expertise in the telelesson:

Thomas Foley–Democrat; U.S. Representative, State of Washington; Speaker of the House
George Fujioki–Internment Camp Detainee
Mollie Fujioki–Internment Camp Detainee
Spark M. Matsunaga–Democrat; U.S. Senator, Hawaii

Telelesson Focus Points

Before viewing the telelesson, read over the following points to help focus your thoughts. After the presentation, write out your responses to help you remember these important points.

1. Who can draft a bill, and who can introduce this legislation?

2. What are the basic steps for a bill to become a law?

3. At which points in the legislative process can an individual influence a bill?

4. How can Congress and the president delay or stop passage of a bill?

5. Why do so few bills become law?

Recommended Reading

The following suggestions are not required reading unless your instructor assigns them. They are listed to let you know where you can find additional information on areas which interest you.

Alter, Jonathan, with Howard Fineman and Eleanor Clift. "World of Congress." *Newsweek* 113, no. 17 (April 24, 1989): pp. 26-34.

Keefe, William J. *The American Legislative Process: Congress and the States*. Englewood Cliffs, N.J.: Prentice-Hall, 1964.

Myer, Dillon S. *Uprooted American: The Japanese-American and the War Relocation Authority during World War II*. Tucson: University of Arizona Press, 1971.

Getting Involved

These activities are not required unless your instructor assigns them. But they offer good suggestions to help you understand and become more involved in the political process.

1. Choose a topic which you believe should be changed by legislation. Contact your state legislators and/or members of Congress about your concern and encourage them to introduce appropriate legislation.

2. Select a topic of interest about which legislation already has been introduced. Locate its present stage and follow the action until it is passed or defeated.

3. If you have access to C-SPAN, watch some of the U.S. House and Senate legislative activities and try to place the action on the legislative-process ladder.

Self Test

After reading the assignment and watching the telelesson, you should be able to answer these questions. When you have completed the test, turn to the Answer Key to score your answers.

1. Before bills can be sent to the president for signing, they must be
   a. signed by the majority leader of each house.
   b. passed by both houses in identical form.
   c. requested by the president.
   d. debated by a joint session of Congress.

2. Congress may override a presidential veto by
   a. an off-the record meeting with the president.
   b. a 51 percent vote in the conference committee.
   c. a two-thirds majority in both houses.
   d. a 51 percent vote in the House.

3. If Congress overrides a presidential veto, the bill
   a. receives a red flag.
   b. carries more importance.
   c. is delayed in implementation.
   d. becomes law without the president's signature.

4. Which of the following statements about the Civil Rights Act of 1991 does NOT illustrate a point about the legislative process?
   a. Declaring the law unconstitutional is the duty of the Supreme Court
   b. A complex issue requires a long time to be resolved
   c. Both sides had to compromise
   d. Interest groups played a part in the process

5. Legislation can be introduced in Congress only by
   a. the president.
   b. lobbyists.
   c. a senator or a representative.
   d. the secretary of state.

6. Once a bill has been introduced in Congress, it is assigned to a
   a. standing committee.
   b. conference committee.
   c. select committee.
   d. joint committee.

7. In which one of the following steps can an individual NOT influence the legislative process?
   a. Introducing the bill on the floor
   b. Testifying before the committee or subcommittee
   c. Lobbying members of Congress
   d. Encouraging the president to sign or veto the bill

8. Debate on a bill in the House is limited and controlled, but the Senate may extend a debate by
   a. requesting a change in a standing committee.
   b. using a filibuster.
   c. adjourning the debate.
   d. postponing a hearing.

Short-Answer Questions:

9. Describe the committee system's effect on the legislative process. Tell why the legislative process takes so long, and why so few bills become law.

10. List some advantages of the long and cumbersome legislative process.

11. The U.S. Constitution requires that both the House and the Senate must pass a particular bill in identical form. Describe how this requirement affects the relationship between the two chambers.

Answer Key

These are the correct answers with reference to the Learning Objectives, and to the source of the information: the Textbook Focus Points, Schmidt, *et al. American Government and Politics Today* (Schmidt), and the Telelesson Focus Points. Page numbers are also given for the Textbook Focus Points. "KT" indicates questions with Key Terms defined.

Question	Answer	Learning Objective	Textbook Focus Point (page no.)	Telelesson Focus Point
1	B	1	1 (Schmidt, p. 411)	
2	C	1	2 (Schmidt, p. 411)............KT	
3	D	1	3 (Schmidt, p. 411)............KT	
4	A	2	4 (Schmidt, p. 414)	
5	C	3		1
6	A	3	4 (Schmidt, p. 411)	2
7	A	4		3
8	B	5	KT	4

Short Answers:

9	5		5
10	5		5
11	1		2,4

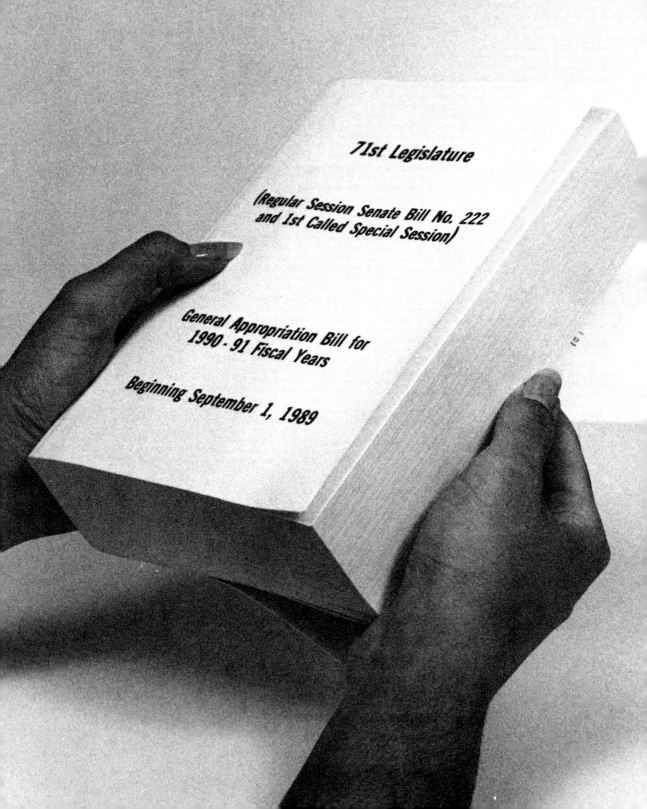

Texas Legislative Process

Overview

Although the governor of Texas is more recognizable than most legislators, and the courts may declare acts of the legislature unconstitutional, the legislative branch is the most powerful of the three branches of Texas state government. The legislature sets state policy about what taxes will be collected, how high the tax rates will be, and how much money each agency can spend to do its job.

This lesson gives you a chance to observe how the state legislature makes a law. The path a bill follows, from its introduction before the state Senate or House of Representatives to when it is signed into law by the governor, is long and complicated. There are many places for it to die, as well as many individuals who influence its content.

Standing committees, influential members, lobbyists, and the speaker of the House and lieutenant governor are all important participants in the Texas legislative process. State senators Kent Caperton, John Montford, and Carl Parker help us by tracing a specific bill, this one on worker's compensation, through the legislative process.

Keep in mind three important facts about the legislative process in Texas: The speaker of the House and the lieutenant governor have enormous power; lobbyists are incredibly influential; and individuals can affect the passage of bills.

The speaker and the lieutenant governor control the fate of bills, by deciding to which committee a bill is assigned. For example, in the Texas House, bills concerning liquor and alcoholic beverages are traditionally assigned to the House Committee on Liquor Regulation.

This committee typically reflects the views of the alcoholic-beverage industry. Should the speaker wish a bill opposed by the alcoholic-beverage industry to be reported out of committee and onto the floor for deliberation, the speaker can refer the bill to the House Committee on State Affairs, which is less likely to reflect the views of the liquor industry. The lieutenant governor exercises similar power in the Senate.

In addition, both the lieutenant governor and the speaker have significant voice in when bills will be debated. So it is not stretching the point to say that few bills are passed without the approval of the speaker and the lieutenant governor.

Lobbyists are representatives of business, church, industry, and other interest and consumer groups. You fulfill the role of a lobbyist if you contact legislators about an issue or visit them in their offices. But most lobbyists are full-time paid professionals, who represent their group's interests in contacts with members of the Texas legislature.

Without doubt, lobbyists are influential because they often contribute money for legislative campaigns, provide food and beverages during legislative sessions, and become friends with various legislators. However, to be effective, lobbyists must be even more influential as a result of the information they possess or can collect: Lobbyists explain to legislators why the legislators should support or oppose bills and how those bills will affect the legislators' constituencies.

So lobbyists' most important assets are their integrity and accurate information. This information is important, because legislative staffs are small and cannot provide legislators with complete information about even the most important bills. Here Billy Clayton, a lobbyist and former speaker of the Texas House of Representatives, describes the importance of lobbying. Brian Dille of Odessa College explains the role of the lobbyist in this process and assesses the impact that individuals can have on lawmaking.

There is a story about the lawmaker who runs up to a lobbyist and says that he cannot support the bill the lobbyist favors, because the legislator has had an avalanche of mail from home in opposition to the bill. An actual count reveals that the lawmaker received six letters!

The point of this story is that individuals, too, can have significant impact on legislation, if they take the time to contact their legislators. Since lawmakers seldom hear from constituents, when constituents do speak up, lawmakers listen.

Individuals also benefit from making time to become informed about issues before the legislature. Many issues directly affect both ourselves and our wallets. Once we understand how the legislative process works, and when and where we can affect it the easiest, it can be a quick and simple matter to make sure our voices are heard.

Learning Objectives

Goal: The purpose of this lesson is to trace the process through which a bill becomes a law in Texas and to illustrate the influence exerted by various constituencies involved in the political process.

Objectives:

1. Explain the four non-legislative powers of the Texas legislature.

2. Differentiate among the types and importance of the various resolutions and bills which reach the Texas legislature.

3. Discuss the influence on Texas lawmaking exerted by the president of the Texas Senate, speaker of the Texas House, governor, attorney general, comptroller of public accounts, and lobbyists.

4. Describe the role of standing committees in the legislative process in Texas, including how compromises and deals are made.

5. List the major steps in the process whereby a bill becomes a law, using legislation on worker's compensation as an example.

6. Evaluate the differing viewpoints concerning the roles of lobbyists and influential groups (e.g., Texas Conservative Coalition) on the legislative process in Texas.

Key Terms

Watch for these terms and pay particular attention to what each one means, as you follow the textbook and telelesson.

General bill   Conference committee
President of the Texas Senate   Lobbying
Speaker of the Texas House   Third House
Standing committee   Caption (TV)
House Research Organization   Workers' compensation
Caucus   legislation (TV)

Textbook Reading Assignment

Jones, Ericson, Brown, and Trotter. *Practicing Texas Politics,* 8th edition. Chapter 6, "The Legislature," pp. 242-297, especially pp. 255-284 and 294-297.

Jones, Ericson, Brown, Trotter, and Lynch. *Practicing Texas Politics – A Brief Survey,* 4th edition. Chapter 6, "The Legislature," pp. 148-188, especially pp. 157-181 and 186-188.

Note To Students: You are responsible for only *one* of the books listed above. It is your responsibility to know which book is used in your class.

Textbook Focus Points

Before you read the textbook assignment, review the following points to help focus your thoughts. After you complete the assignment, write your responses to reinforce what you have learned.

1. What are the four non-legislative powers of the Texas legislature?

2. What are the differences among simple resolutions, concurrent resolutions, and joint resolutions? Which type of resolution is most important?

3. What are the differences between special bills, local bills, bracket bills, and general bills?

4. What are the formal powers of the president of the Texas Senate and speaker of the Texas House of Representatives?

5. What are the duties of House and Senate standing committees? How are their members appointed? How are their chairpersons selected? How do standing committees influence the passage of legislation?

6. What are the major concerns of the House Research Organization, party caucuses, Texas Conservative Coalition, Legislative Black Caucus, and Mexican-American Legislative Caucus?

7. What are the major steps in how a bill becomes law? Which steps allow individuals the greatest opportunity to influence proposed legislation?

8. How do the governor, attorney general, comptroller of public accounts, and lobbyists influence the legislative process?

Telelesson Interviewees

The following individuals will share their expertise in the telelesson:

Kent Caperton–Member, Texas Senate, Bryan
Billy Clayton–Lobbyist
Brian Dille–Department of Government, Odessa College
Molly Ivins–Columnist and Author
John Montford–Member, Texas Senate, Lubbock
Carl Parker–Member, Texas Senate, Beaumont-Port Arthur

Telelesson Focus Points

Before viewing the telelesson, read the following points to help focus your thoughts. After the presentation, write your responses to help you remember these important points.

1. Which two elected officials have the most control over the legislative process? What gives them this power?

2. Where in the legislative process are deals or compromises on legislation most likely to be made?

3. What control does the governor have over the legislative process?

4. What were the issues involved in the reform of the workers' compensation system in Texas? Which two powerful groups opposed each other on this issue?

5. What is the roll of the lobbyist in the legislative process? How much influence do lobbyists have in the legislative process?

6. To what extent do Billy Clayton and Molly Ivins differ on the legislative process and the role of lobbyists in that process?

Recommended Reading

The following suggestions are not required unless your instructor assigns them. They are listed to let you know where you can find additional information on areas which interest you.

Denison, Dave. "Trickle-Down Legislation." *Texas Observer* (April 5, 1986): pp. 2-5.

How the Texas Legislature Works. Dallas: Texas Women's Commission Foundation, 1987.

Ivins, Molly. *Molly Ivins Can't Say That, Can She?.* New York: Random House, 1991.

Rips, Geoffrey. "The Battle for Farmworker Compensation." *Texas Observer* (January 13, 1984): pp. 7-15.

Texas Legislative Handbook. Austin: Texas State Directory, Inc., published biannually.

Texas Legislative Manual. Austin: Texas State Directory, Inc., 1984.

Zaffirini, Senator Judith. "One Senator's Social Agenda." *Texas Journal of Political Studies,* 10 (Fall/Winter 1987-1988): pp. 31-34.

Getting Involved

These activities are not required unless your instructor assigns them. But they offer good suggestions to help you understand and become more involved in the political process.

1. Learn the names and addresses of your state representative and state senator. Write them on an issue that concerns you.

2. When the legislature is in session, select a topic of interest that the legislature is considering. Find its present location in the legislative process and follow the bill until it is passed or defeated.

Self Test

After reading the assignment and watching the telelesson, you should be able to answer these questions. When you have completed the test, turn to the Answer Key to score your answers.

1. Impeachment
   a. requires a simple majority vote of the Texas Senate.
   b. involves bringing charges against a person.
   c. mandates removal from office.
   d. requires a two-thirds vote of the Texas House.

2. The power which allows one chamber of the Texas legislature to influence the selection of officials of the executive branch is its
   a. constitutional amendment power.
   b. impeachment power.
   c. investigative power.
   d. control over administration.

3. Impeachment charges against an individual are made by the Texas
   a. House of Representatives and the trial takes place in the Texas Senate.
   b. Senate and the trial takes place in the Texas House of Representatives.
   c. House of Representatives and the trial takes place in the Texas Supreme Court.
   d. Senate and the trial takes place in the Texas Supreme Court.

4. A resolution which requires the action of only one house of the Texas legislature and may deal with rules of the Texas House or Senate is a
   a. simple resolution.
   b. concurrent resolution.
   c. joint resolution.
   d. legislative resolution.

5. A resolution which grants an individual permission to sue the state, and requires the action of both houses of the Texas legislature and the signature of the governor, is a
   a. simple resolution.
   b. concurrent resolution.
   c. joint resolution.
   d. legislative resolution.

6. A bill which affects all people or property in Texas is a
   a. bracket bill.
   b. general bill.
   c. local bill.
   d. special bill.

7. In Texas, a bill which grants an exception to general laws for the benefit of an individual, class or corporation is a
   a. bracket bill.
   b. general bill.
   c. local bill.
   d. special bill.

8. The presiding officer of the Texas Senate is the
   a. lieutenant governor.
   b. speaker of the Senate.
   c. president pro tempore of the Senate.
   d. majority leader of the Senate.

9. The presiding officer of the Texas House of Representatives is the
   a. lieutenant governor.
   b. speaker of the House.
   c. majority leader of the House.
   d. president pro tempore of the House.

10. In Texas, the speaker of the House controls standing committees by
    a. serving as governor when the governor and lieutenant governor are absent from the state.
    b. participating as an ex-officio member when issues warrant such influence.
    c. appointing one-half of the membership of each standing committee and appointing its chairperson.
    d. setting the committee's agenda.

11. Committees which control the fate of bills introduced into the Texas legislature are
    a. standing committees.
    b. conference committees.
    c. special committees.
    d. procedural committees.

12. In the Texas Senate, chairpersons of standing committees are
    a. elected by the membership of the committee.
    b. elected by the membership of the Senate.
    c. appointed by the majority leader.
    d. appointed by the lieutenant governor.

13. In Texas, the group that publishes the *Daily Floor Report*, which analyzes important bills by providing objective summaries of their contents and arguments for and against passage, is the
    a. Office of the Speaker.
    b. Office of the Secretary of the House.
    c. House Research Organization.
    d. House Analysis Group.

14. A meeting of like-minded legislators is called a
    a. caucus.
    b. corresponding meeting.
    c. coalition.
    d. recess gathering.

15. In Texas, the caucus which placed farm workers under the unemployment compensation program and insured them minimum wage protection is the
    a. House Study Group.
    b. Senate Republican Caucus.
    c. Texas Conservative Coalition.
    d. Mexican-American Legislative Caucus.

16. A bill passed in different forms by the Texas House and Senate is sent to a
    a. special committee.
    b. standing committee.
    c. conference committee.
    d. standing special committee.

17. In Texas, the governor can influence legislation by
    a. discharging a conference committee within fifteen days of its appointment.
    b. threatening to veto legislation.
    c. exercising a pocket veto.
    d. appointing friends and associates as chairpersons of interim legislative study groups.

18. Providing information for legislators and serving as links to organized groups of constituents is
    a. lobbying.
    b. log rolling.
    c. pork-barrel politics.
    d. illegal.

19. Because of their influence on public policy, Austin's lobbyists are referred to as the
    a. policy kings.
    b. fourth estate.
    c. first team.
    d. third house.

20. The two officials who have the most control over the legislative process in Texas are the
    a. governor and the lieutenant governor.
    b. governor and comptroller of public accounts.
    c. lieutenant governor and the speaker of the Texas House.
    d. speaker of the Texas House and the attorney general.

21. In the legislative process in Texas, most bargains or compromises on bills are made
    a. in special committee.
    b. in standing committee.
    c. on the floor of the Texas House or Senate.
    d. after being forwarded to the governor.

22. The governor's power to influence the legislative process includes the ability to
    a. exercise an item veto.
    b. introduce bills into the legislature.
    c. call no more than three special sessions every two years.
    d. discharge the legislature between day 121 and day 140 of its regular session.

23. Each bill introduced into the Texas legislature contains a brief explanation of its contents, which is called
    a. an introductory clause.
    b. an enabling clause.
    c. a caption.
    d. an interpretative clause.

24. Workers' compensation statutes in Texas needed to be reformed because the
    a. premiums were high and the benefits were relatively low.
    b. decisions of federal courts declared Texas' statutes unconstitutional.
    c. Sunset Review Commission had recommended abolishment of the current system.
    d. governor had vetoed a previous revision of workers' compensation legislation.

25. Most experts agree that lobbyists in Texas have
    a. little influence over what laws are passed.
    b. declined in influence in the past ten years.
    c. declined in number, but increased in influence.
    d. a major role in the legislative process.

Short-Answer Question:

26. Contrast the view that Billy Clayton offers of the legislative process and lobbyists with the view offered by Molly Ivins.

Answer Key

These are the correct answers with reference to the Learning Objectives, and to the source of the information: the Textbook Focus Points, Jones, *et al. Practicing Texas Politics* (Jones) or Jones, *et. al., Practicing Texas Politics — A Brief Survey* (Survey); the Study Guide Overview (Overview); and the Telelesson Focus Points. Page numbers are also given for the Textbook Focus Points. "KT" indicates questions with Key Terms defined.

Question	Answer	Learning Objective	Textbook Focus Point (page no.)	Telelesson Focus Point
1	B	1	1 (Jones, p. 258; Survey, p. 160)	
2	D	1	1 (Jones, pp. 257-258; Survey, pp. 159-160)	
3	A	1	1 (Jones, p. 258; Survey, p. 160)	
4	A	2	2 (Jones, p. 256; Survey, p. 158)	
5	B	2	2 (Jones, p. 256; Survey, p. 158)	
6	B	2	3 (Jones, pp. 256-257; Survey, pp. 158-159)	KT
7	D	2	3 (Jones, pp. 256-257; Survey, pp. 158-159)	
8	A	3	4 (Jones, p. 260; Survey, p. 161)	KT
9	B	3	4 (Jones, pp. 261-263; Survey, pp. 162-165)	KT
10	C	3	4 (Jones, pp. 261-263; Survey, pp. 162-165)	
11	A	4	5 (Jones, p. 263; Survey, p. 165)	KT
12	D	4	5 (Jones, pp. 263-266; Survey, pp. 165-167)	
13	C	6	6 (Jones, p. 266; Survey, p. 168)	KT
14	A	6	6 (Jones, p. 266; Survey, p. 169)	KT
15	D	6	6 (Jones, p. 268; Survey, p. 170)	
16	C	5	7 (Jones, pp. 270-273; Survey, pp. 172-175)	KT
17	B	3	8 (Jones, pp. 273-274; Survey, p. 175)	
18	A	3	8 (Jones, pp. 275-276; Survey, pp. 177-178)	KT
19	D	3	8 (Jones, p. 276; Survey, p. 178)	KT
20	C	3		1
21	B	4		2
22	A	3		3
23	C	5		2
24	A	5		4
25	D	6		5

Short Answer:

26		6		6

Lesson 5

The President and Congress

Overview

This lesson is one of a series of lessons on the Congress, the legislative process, and the presidency. Here we examine the deliberate and intentional conflict between the legislative and executive branches of government, and how it gets resolved.

The founders knew that the "checks and balances" which they built into the U.S. Constitution would mean a continuous battle for power and control. But they believed the struggle would be worth it in order to prevent one branch from becoming stronger than another.

Consequently, the conflict between Congress and the president is a natural outgrowth of our constitutional system. The president represents the entire nation and must look at national needs and concerns, whereas members of Congress represent a state, or a district within a state, and therefore offer a narrower geographical and socioeconomic perspective.

The checks and balances work like this: One constitutional role of the president is commander in chief, but only Congress can declare war. Congress makes all of the laws, but the president may veto them. The president may negotiate and sign a treaty, but the treaty is not valid unless the Senate approves (ratifies) it. The president appoints ambassadors, judges and cabinet officials, but they don't take office until the Senate consents to these appointments.

With all the conflict designed into the system, we may wonder what prevents a stalemate, a government that cannot act at all. The answer is that out of conflict comes some form of cooperation. Conflict causes Congress and the president to analyze the issues more closely, to maintain their stands on those provisions that are in what they perceive to be our best interests, and to discard those that might be less important or carry more risk.

In this lesson we look at two examples of conflict and cooperation: the budgetary responsibility and the war-making power. In the process we examine the powers that the Constitution gives each branch and see how both branches compromise to make our government work.

Learning Objectives

Goal: The purpose of "The President and Congress" is to illustrate the cooperation and conflict intentionally designed into the relationship between the legislative and executive branches of the U.S. government.

Objectives:

1. Outline the cooperative relationship and potential conflict between the president and Congress, as the president performs the constitutional roles of commander in chief, chief diplomat, and chief legislator.

2. Describe how special uses of presidential power create conflict between the president and Congress, particularly the Senate.

3. Illustrate conflict between the president and Congress, using the constitutional bases for budgetary responsibilities and war powers as examples, then show how the battles were resolved.

4. Explain the rationale of the founders in building conflict between the president and Congress into our governmental system.

Key Terms

Watch for these terms and pay particular attention to what each one means, as you follow the textbook and telelesson.

War Powers Act   **Executive privilege**
Advice and consent   **Impeachment**
Executive agreements   **Impoundment (TV)**
Veto message

Textbook Reading Assignment

Schmidt, Shelley, and Bardes. *American Government and Politics Today*, 1993-94 edition. Chapter 12, "The Congress," and Chapter 13, "The Presidency." [Review both chapters. In Chapter 12, focus on pp. 380-381, 410-416. In Chapter 13, pay particular attention to pp. 425-426, 429-443, 445-448.]

Textbook Focus Points

Before you read the textbook assignment, review the following points to help focus your thoughts. After you complete the assignment, write out your responses to reinforce what you have learned.

1. How has the War Powers Act affected the relationship between Congress and the president (as commander in chief)?

2. Where might conflict arise between Congress and the president when the president is performing the role of chief diplomat?

3. Where does conflict erupt between Congress and the president (as chief legislator)?

4. How can special uses of presidential power create conflict between Congress and the president?

Telelesson Interviewees

The following individuals share their expertise in the telelesson:

Thomas E. Cronin–Professor of Political Science, The Colorado College

William Gray–Democrat; Former U.S. Representative, Pennsylvania; Majority Whip; Former Chair of House Budget Committee

Andrea Mitchell–Chief Congressional Correspondent, NBC News

Charles Percy–Republican; Former Senator, Illinois

Elliot Richardson–Cabinet Member and Ambassador, Nixon and Ford Administrations

Telelesson Focus Points

Before viewing the telelesson, read over the following points to help focus your thoughts. After the presentation, write out your responses to help you remember these important points.

1. Why is there a conflict between Congress and the president over the budget?

2. What particularly causes conflict between the president and the Senate?

3. How can war-making powers create a conflict between the president and Congress?

4. Why was the conflict between the president and Congress built into our governmental system?

Recommended Reading

The following suggestions are not required unless your instructor assigns them. They are listed to let you know where you can find additional information on areas which interest you.

Borger, Gloria. "Storming the Tower." *U.S. News & World Report* 106 (March 6, 1989): pp. 37-39.

Cronin, Thomas E. *The State of the Presidency*, 2nd edition. Boston: Little, Brown, 1980.

Kernell, Samuel. *Going Public: New Strategies of Presidential Leadership*. Washington, D.C.: Congressional Quarterly Press, 1986.

Lamar, Jacob V. "Gone With the Wind." *Time* 130 (October 12, 1987): pp. 18-20.

Morganthau, T. "Tower's Troubles." *Newsweek* 113 (March 6, 1989): pp. 16-20+.

Press, Aric. "Bork in the Balance." *Newsweek* 110 (October 12, 1987): pp. 38-40.

Smith, Hedrick. "Divided Government: Gridlock and the Blame Game" in *The Power Game*. New York: Random House, 1988, pp. 651-667.

Getting Involved

These activities are not required unless your instructor assigns them. But they offer good suggestions to help you understand and become more involved in the political process.

1. In 1987 President Reagan nominated Robert Bork to the U.S. Supreme Court. This nomination encountered great opposition in the Senate and ultimately was defeated. Research Judge Bork's nomination and the Senate confirmation hearings: Who opposed the nomination and why? How did the administration react to the opposition? Pay careful attention to the conflict that arose when the president and Congress each performed their constitutional duties.

2. Select either the Special Watergate Committee of 1973 or the action by the House Judiciary Committee on articles of impeachment against President Richard Nixon in 1974. Examine news reports and books by participants. Look for the various points of conflict between the president and Congress.

Self Test

After reading the assignment and watching the telelesson, you should be able to answer these questions. When you have completed the test, turn to the Answer Key to score your answers.

1. In spite of the passage of the War Powers Act, the power of the president as commander in chief is
   a. virtually destroyed, with all real power belonging to the Joint Chiefs of Staff.
   b. much stronger than if it had not passed.
   c. increased, unless Congress declares war and takes control of the military.
   d. more extensive today than at any other time in our history.

2. The treaties negotiated and the ambassadors appointed by the president are worthless without
   a. diplomatic recognition by foreign powers.
   b. executive agreements with heads of foreign states.
   c. a State of the Union message by the president.
   d. the advice and consent of the Senate.

3. If the president uses a regular veto, the president must
   a. submit legislation that would accomplish the same goal through a different means.
   b. avoid using another regular veto for ten working days.
   c. obtain the approval of the majority leader in the Senate and the speaker of the House.
   d. return the bill to Congress with a veto message.

4. Presidents have at their disposal a variety of special powers and privileges which
   a. are not available to the other branches of U.S. government.
   b. have been carefully used with great discretion.
   c. Congress has tried to usurp.
   d. have been flaunted before Congress.

5. The Constitution specifically grants Congress the power to collect taxes, pay debts, and borrow money, whereas the president has
   a. sole responsibility for preparing the national budget.
   b. relinquished budgetary responsibility to Congress.
   c. no specific, constitutional, budgetary duties.
   d. always worked closely with Congress in developing a budget.

6. The Senate can assert itself over the president through
   a. denying the appointment of a federal judge.
   b. investigating the impeachment of a president.
   c. vetoing a president's proposal.
   d. impounding appropriated funds.

7. The War Powers Act has the effect of
   a. increasing the power and maneuverability of the president.
   b. decreasing the power and maneuverability of the president.
   c. making it easier for the president to work with Congress.
   d. making Congress appreciate the difficult job of being president.

8. According to Charles Percy, the founders wanted the president and Congress to share powers in order to
   a. protect the people and remove the possibility of autocracy.
   b. generate an attitude of cooperation among all the states.
   c. create a sense of "unitedness" among the individual states.
   d. stimulate a thorough examination of the issues before setting policies.

Short-Answer Question:
   9. Do you believe that Congress should place constraints on the president? Why or why not?

Answer Key

These are the correct answers with reference to the Learning Objectives, and to the source of the information: the Textbook Focus Points, Schmidt, *et al. American Government and Politics Today* (Schmidt), and the Telelesson Focus Points. Page numbers are also given for the Textbook Focus Points. "KT" indicates questions with Key Terms defined.

Question	Answer	Learning Objective	Textbook Focus Point (page no.)	Telelesson Focus Point
1	D	1	1 (Schmidt, p. 434)............KT	
2	D	1	2 (Schmidt, p. 434)............KT	
3	D	1	3 (Schmidt, p. 439)............KT	
4	A	2	4 (Schmidt, p. 449)	
5	C	3		1
6	A	2	2 (Schmidt, p. 431)	2
7	B	3	1 (Schmidt, p. 434)............KT	3
8	A	4		4

Short Answer:

9		4	1,2,3,4 (Schmidt, pp. 427-443)	1,2,3,4

Lesson 6

Philosophies of Representation

Overview

During a campaign, candidates promise the voters to work for their state's or district's interests. As members of a political party, candidates are pledged to support that party's platform. Yet candidates receive most of the money to run their campaigns from individuals and political action committees. For whom, then, does the politician speak? Who does the elected official really represent?

Even more important, once the candidate is elected, how should that person vote? Should he or she vote the way most of the people in the district want, for what the political party wants, or in the best interests of the state or nation? Or, should that person vote for the issues supported by the individuals and groups who contributed to the campaign?

There are two competing theories of representation: the delegate theory and the trustee theory. Politicians who advocate the delegate theory believe they are bound to represent the majority of their constituents. They see themselves as delegates, simply with instructions from the "home folks" on how to vote on critical issues. They reflect the wishes of their constituents.

The trustee theory of representation was advocated by Edmund Burke, a member of the British Parliament. Politicians who view themselves as trustees believe that they are elected to vote in the best interests of the nation, state, or district, with little regard to what the "home folks" want. Supporters of this position assume they have more complete information and greater experience than the people back home. Therefore, they should vote on the basis of this information and experience, not simply for what is expected of them by the voters.

In reality, few lawmakers act consistently as either delegates or trustees. Some political scientists have conceived the term "politico" for the legislative role which combines both the delegate and the trustee concepts. In this role, the lawmaker chooses between the two philosophies based on the specific issue being considered.

For example, the Seventeenth Congressional District in Texas encompasses a large geographic area but only one large city, Abilene. Oil, natural gas, grain crops, cotton, and dairy cattle are important economically. The U.S. Representative from this area may operate as a trustee, voting in the best interests of the state or nation on issues affecting metropolitan areas and foreign affairs, but chooses a delegate role, voting the wishes of the constituency on issues affecting the district like domestic oil production and milk-price supports. By combining the roles of trustee and delegate, this representative becomes what we call a politico.

The video portion of this lesson more fully explores the roles of delegate, trustee, and politico. Members of the Texas legislature and U.S. House of Representatives describe how they seek to represent their constituents and still keep the best interests of the state and nation in mind. Sociologist Deborah Wood examines how individuals acquire their attitudes about government and politics, then how these attitudes affect their political participation. John Forshee, a political scientist, describes what happens when politicians no longer represent the real views of their constituents.

Learning Objectives

Goal: The purpose of this lesson is to differentiate among philosophies of representation categorized as delegate, trustee, and politico.

Objectives:

1. Describe the theories of representation known as delegate, trustee, and politico.

2. Contrast the voting strategies of legislators representing the delegate, trustee, and politico theories of representation.

3. Categorize the philosophies of specific legislators according to one of the theories of representation.

Key Terms

Watch for these terms and pay particular attention to what each one means, as you follow the textbook and telelesson.

Delegate theory of representation (Overview)
Trustee theory of representation (Overview)
Politico (Overview)
Political socialization (TV)

Textbook Reading Assignment

There is no textbook reading assignment for this lesson. Be sure to read the overview to this lesson carefully.

Telelesson Interviewees

The following individuals will share their expertise in the telelesson:

John Bryant–Member, U.S. House of Representatives, Dallas

Eddie Cavazos–Member, Texas House of Representatives, Corpus Christi

Wilhelmina Delco–Member, Texas House of Representatives, Austin

John Forshee–Dallas County Community College District

Carlos Truan–Member, Texas Senate, Corpus Christi

Deborah Wood–Dallas County Community College District

Telelesson Focus Points

Before viewing the telelesson, read the following points to help focus your thoughts. After the presentation, write your responses to help you remember these important points.

1. What are the differences among legislators who reflect the delegate, trustee, or politico theory of representation?

2. What factors determine how a legislator votes?

3. To which theory of representation do John Bryant, Eddie Cavazos, Wilhelmina Delco, and Carlos Truan subscribe?

Recommended Reading

There are no recommended readings for this lesson.

Getting Involved

This activity is not required unless your instructor assigns it. But it offers good suggestions to help you understand and become more involved in the political process.

> Identify your state representative, state senator, U.S. representative, or U.S. senator. Follow this person's public statements and votes on several issues. Write a brief essay identifying this person as a delegate, trustee, or politico.

Self Test

After reading the assignment and watching the telelesson, you should be able to answer these questions. When you have completed the test, turn to the Answer Key to score your answers.

1. Representatives who reflect their constituents' views are known as
   a. delegates.
   b. trustees.
   c. politicos.
   d. uninformed.

2. Most elected officials tend to be
   a. delegates.
   b. trustees.
   c. politicos.
   d. familiar.

3. Which of the following is NOT a major factor in determining how an individual will vote once elected to office?
   a. Educational background
   b. Religious background
   c. Ethnic background
   d. Size of district represented

4. The way in which an individual acquires attitudes and beliefs about government and politics is
   a. of little importance to the study of government and politics.
   b. political socialization.
   c. social politicalization.
   d. dual electioneering.

5. According to John Forshee, the effect of a representative's constituents on voting is of
   a. extreme importance, since reelection depends on voting record.
   b. great value, because many constituents make their views known on most issues.
   c. less consequence than many people believe, because few constituents make their views known.
   d. almost no importance on most issues.

6. The philosophy of representation of such elected officials as John Bryant, Eddi Cavazos, Wilhelmina Delco, and Carlos Truan is known as
   a. delegate.
   b. trustee.
   c. politico.
   d. socialized.

Answer Key

These are the correct answers with reference to the Learning Objectives, and to the source of the information: the Textbook Focus Points, Jones, *et al. Practicing Texas Politics* (Jones) or Jones, *et. al., Practicing Texas Politics — A Brief Survey* (Survey); the Study Guide Overview (Overview); and the Telelesson Focus Points. Page numbers are also given for the Textbook Focus Points. "KT" indicates questions with Key Terms defined.

Question	Answer	Learning Objective	Textbook Focus Point (page no.)	Telelesson Focus Point
1	A	1		1
2	C	1		1
3	D	2		2
4	B	2		2
5	C	2		2
6	C	3		3

Lesson 7

The Presidency

Overview

Now it is time to add a second branch, the executive branch, to the three-branch structure of U.S. government. The president is head of the executive branch, which executes (administers or carries out) the laws passed by Congress, the legislative branch.

The executive branch is composed of the president, vice president, the president's cabinet, the Executive Office of the President, numerous independent regulatory agencies, and government corporations. (Another lesson will delve more into the plethora of government departments and agencies, as it describes the bureaucracy.)

Article II of the U.S. Constitution gives the president five powers: chief of state, chief executive, commander in chief, chief diplomat, and chief legislator. In addition to these five constitutional powers, the president is expected to fulfill several responsibilities just because he or she is president and the office requires it; these are called "inherent powers." We expect one individual to fulfill all the presidential roles, and we judge presidential success or failure by how well each president performs these roles.

Yet as our nation and our world have grown in size and complexity, being president of the United States has become much more difficult. Today, many people also consider it the most powerful position in the world. But, as a result of the almost superhuman challenges of the position, it is just about impossible for any one person to succeed in every area, or even to excel in several areas. What we have discovered is that some presidents will have great success performing one role, such as chief legislator, and fail in another, such as commander in chief.

Also due to the tremendous complexity of the job, presidents usually choose to emphasize one or two roles, and this choice influences the way they handle the job. Presidents cannot make decisions unchecked, for the founders designed a system of checks and balances to prevent one branch from becoming stronger than any other. However, this system creates conflict among the three branches, particularly between Congress and the president, which will be examined in the next lesson.

We as a nation are quick to criticize both presidential successes and presidential failures. On one hand we claim (or complain) that the presidency has become too powerful. On the other hand we say that the presidency is too weak. The more we learn about this massive job, the better able we become to evaluate what any one president does, and to cast our votes for the person best fitted to serve our nation at a particular time.

Learning Objectives

Goal: The purpose of "The Presidency" is to describe the organization and powers of the Executive Branch and to assess why a president will choose to emphasize one role over another.

Objectives:

1. Describe the constitutional requirements and personal considerations of individuals who aspire to become president of the United States.

2. List and explain the roles of the president, including acting as party chief, super politician, and television personality.

3. Discuss ways that presidents emphasize various roles and powers, using Lyndon Johnson and Jimmy Carter as examples.

4. Explain the impeachment process.

5. Describe the support the president receives from the Executive Office and the vice president.

6. Explain the high expectations the public holds for the president and the effect of these expectations on presidential performance.

7. Recount Helen Thomas's description of the presidency today and how the media have changed their coverage of the president.

8. Cite your opinion with supporting rationale as to whether the power of the presidency is increasing or decreasing.

Key Terms

Watch for these terms and pay particular attention to what each one means, as you follow the textbook and telelesson.

Chief of state	Emergency powers
Chief executive	Executive order
Appointment power	Executive privilege
Commander in Chief	Impeachment
Chief diplomat	Cabinet
Executive agreements	Executive Office of the President
Chief legislator	White House Office
State of the Union message	Council of Economic Advisers
Constitutional powers	Office of Management and Budget
Statutory powers	National Security Council
Express powers	Twenty-fifth Amendment
Inherent powers	

Textbook Reading Assignment

Schmidt, Shelley, and Bardes. *American Government and Politics Today*, 1993-94 edition. Chapter 13, "The Presidency," pp. 423-461.

Textbook Focus Points

Before you read the textbook assignment, review the following points to help focus your thoughts. After you complete the assignment, write out your responses to reinforce what you have learned.

1. What are the qualifications to become president of the United States?

2. What are the five constitutional roles of the president and the functions of each?

3. In addition to the constitutional powers, what other powers does the president have?

4. What are the president's duties as party chief and super politician?

5. In what special ways have presidents used their powers?

6. How does the impeachment process work?

7. How is the Executive Office of the President organized?

8. How has the role of vice president as advisor and successor to the president evolved?

Telelesson Interviewees

The following individuals share their expertise in the telelesson:

George Christian–Former Press Secretary, Johnson Administration

Stuart Eizenstat–Chief Domestic Policy Advisor, Carter Administration

Kenneth Janda–Professor of Political Science, Northwestern University

Ron Nessen–Former Press Secretary, Ford Administration

Jody Powell–Former Press Secretary, Carter Administration

Helen Thomas–UPI White House Bureau Chief

Telelesson Focus Points

Before viewing the telelesson, read over the following points to help focus your thoughts. After the presentation, write out your responses to help you remember these important points.

1. Why does the public expect too much from the president, and how do these expectations influence how a president performs?

2. According to Jody Powell and Ron Nesson, what should the public realistically expect from a president, and why can't the president meet these expectations?

3. What roles did Lyndon Johnson and Jimmy Carter emphasize, and why?

4. How has television affected the presidency?

5. How does Helen Thomas describe both the presidency and how the media have changed in their coverage of the president?

6. Is the power of the presidency increasing or decreasing?

Recommended Reading

The following suggestions are not required unless your instructor assigns them. They are listed to let you know where you can find additional information on areas which interest you.

Barber, James David. *Presidential Character*, 3rd edition. Englewood Cliffs, N.J.: Prentice-Hall, 1985.

Cronin, Thomas E. "An Imperiled Presidency" in *The Post-Imperial Presidency*, Vincent Davis, editor. New Brunswick, N.J.: Transaction Books, 1980.

Schlesinger, Arthur. *The Imperial Presidency*. Boston: Houghton Mifflin, 1973.

Smith, Hedrick. "The Presidency and the Power Float: Our Rotating Prime Ministers" in *The Power Game*. New York: Random House, 1988, pp. 3-19.

Getting Involved

These activities are not required unless your instructor assigns them. But they offer good suggestions to help you understand and become more involved in the political process.

1. Note the "Getting Involved" section of your textbook at the end of Chapter 13.

2. Select a biography of a twentieth-century president. Read it to determine in which roles this person achieved the most success and in which roles, the least. Because of these successes and failures, did your opinion of this person change? Why?

Self Test

After reading the assignment and watching the telelesson, you should be able to answer these questions. When you have completed the test, turn to the Answer Key to score your answers.

1. Which of the following is NOT a constitutional requirement for becoming president of the United States?
   a. Must be a natural-born citizen
   b. Must be at least 35-years old
   c. Must have held an elective office
   d. Must have been a U.S. resident for 14 years

2. Which of the following is NOT a constitutional power of the president?
   a. Chief of state
   b. Chief of party
   c. Commander in chief
   d. Chief diplomat

Replace Question #16 with:

16. A major problem, concerning age groups, is going to be the vast increase in the number of
    a. people reaching retirement age within a twenty-year period.
    b. college-age students for the next ten years.
    c. children attending public schools.
    d. discriminatory hiring practices affecting older citizens.

(The correct answer is A.)

Replace Question #19 with:

19. In July 1993, President Bill Clinton announced a new policy, referred to as, "don't ask, don't tell," which would
    a. prohibit gay males and lesbians from serving in the military.
    b. allow gay males and lesbians to serve in the military as long as they did not commit homosexual acts.
    c. prevent state governments from passing discriminatory legislation affecting gay males and lesbians.
    d. view sexual conduct as a state concern over which the U.S. Supreme Court had no jurisdiction.

(The correct answer is B.)

Revised page numbers in the **Answer Key**:

1.	p. 147	8.	p. 168	15.	p. 193
2.	pp. 149-150	9.	p. 172	16.	p. 198
3.	p. 151	10.	p. 175	17.	p. 202
4.	p. 155	11.	p. 176	18.	p. 205
5.	p. 159	12.	p. 185	19.	p. 211
6.	p. 161	13.	p. 188	20-26.	No change
7.	p. 167	14.	p. 192		

Short Answer:
27. pp. 175-177
28. No change

LESSON 21--INDIVIDUAL RIGHTS

Revised **Textbook Reading Assignment**: pp. 109-112, 127-134.

Revised page numbers in the **Answer Key**:

1. p. 109	4. p. 111	6. p. 130
2. p. 110	5. p. 129	7-13. No change
3. p. 110		

Short Answer:
14. pp. 127-129

LESSON 23--FIRST AMENDMENT FREEDOMS

Revised **Textbook Reading Assignment**: pp. 112-129

Revised page numbers in the **Answer Key**:

1. p. 112	5. p. 122	9. No change
2. p. 115	6. p. 127	10. p. 116
3. p. 115	7. No change	11. p. 113
4. p. 120	8. No change	12-15. No change

LESSON 25--WOMEN AND MINORITIES

Revised **Textbook Reading Assignment**: pp. 145-182 and pp.183-216.

Revised **Self Test**:
Replace Question #14 with:
14. After Congress proposed the Equal Rights Amendment in 1972, it was
    a. opposed by over 65% of the public.
    b. held to be unconstitutional by the Supreme Court in the case of ROE V. WADE in 1973.
    c. perceived to have tremendous popular support.
    d. rejected by 35 states within two years.
                    (The correct answer is C.)

LESSON 15--THE JUDICIARY

Revised **Textbook Reading Assignment**: pp. 519-534, 545-553.

Revised page numbers in the **Answer Key**:
- 1. p. 521
- 2. pp. 521-522
- 3. pp. 522-523
- 4. p. 526
- 5. pp. 529-530
- 6. p. 530
- 7. p. 545
- 8-14. No change

Short Answer:
- 15. pp. 529-534

LESSON 17--THE JUDICIAL SELECTION PROCESS

Revised **Textbook Reading Assignment**: pp. 534-545.

Revised page numbers in the **Answer Key**:
- 1. p. 535
- 2. p. 537
- 3. p. 537
- 4. p. 539
- 5. p. 544
- 6. No change
- 7. No change
- 8. No change
- 9. No change
- 10. p. 535
- 11-12. No change

LESSON 19--RIGHTS OF THE ACCUSED

Revised **Textbook Reading Assignment**: pp. 108, 134-144.

Revised page numbers in the **Answer Key**:
- 1. p. 134
- 2. p. 134
- 3. p. 135
- 4. p. 135
- 5. p. 136
- 6. p. 136
- 7. p. 137
- 8. No change
- 9. No change
- 10. p. 137
- 11. No change
- 12. No change
- 13. p. 136
- 14. p. 135
- 15. p. 136

Short Answer:
- 16. pp. 134-137

Revised **Self Test**:

Replace Question #3 with:

3. Because of the aging of the population and the increased use of technology that is more expensive, the percentage of national income going to health care
   a. will be decreased before new tests are implemented.
   b. can be expected to rise no matter what kind of plan is put into place.
   c. can only encourage young doctors to enter specialized fields.
   d. will be excluded from national income tax deductions.

   (The correct answer is B.)

Replace Question #6 with:

6. What provision was NOT included in the Violent Crime Control and Law Enforcement Act of 1994?
   a. Increased resources for law
   b. "Three-strikes-and-you're-out" sentencing
   c. Federal funding for community education programs
   d. Ban on assault weapons

   (The correct answer is C.)

Revised page numbers in the **Answer Key**:

1. p. 561	4. pp. 584-585	6. p. 571
2. p. 572	5. p. 564	7-12. No change
3. p. 573		

Short Answer:

13. pp. 559-561

LESSON 13--FOREIGN POLICY

Revised **Textbook Reading Assignment**: pp. 623-657.

Revised page numbers in the **Answer Key**:

1. p. 625	4. p. 629	7. pp. 636-638
2. p. 626	5. p. 633	8. p. 641
3. p. 628	6. p. 633	9-17. No change

Revised page numbers in the **Answer Key**:

1. p. 454	4. p. 465	7. p. 454
2. p. 455	5. No change	8. No change
3. p. 459	6. p. 455	

Short Answer:
9. pp. 449-462

LESSON 7--THE PRESIDENCY

Revised **Textbook Reading Assignment**: pp. 443-483.

Revised page numbers in the **Answer Key**:

1. p. 445	4. p. 463	7. pp. 469-472
2. p. 449	5. p. 464	8. p. 474
3. p. 462	6. p. 468	9-13. No change

Short Answer:
14. No text reference

LESSON 9--THE BUREAUCRACY

Revised **Textbook Reading Assignment**: pp. 485-516.

Revised page numbers in the **Answer Key**:

1. p. 487	4. p. 499	7. p. 511
2. p. 487	5. p. 502	8-15. No change
3. p. 491	6. p. 508	

LESSON 11--DOMESTIC POLICY

Revised **Key Terms**:
Add "Domestic policy"

Revised **Textbook Reading Assignment**: pp. 557-594. Delete reference to Chapter 17.

REVISIONS--GOVERNMENT BY CONSENT II (Dallas Version)
for the
Telecourse Study Guide for Government by Consent II
Executive, Legislative and Judicial Branches
3rd Edition
by Lee, Forshee, Lynch
when used with the **1995-96 Edition** of the Textbook,
American Government and Politics Today by Schmidt, Shelly, Bardes

LESSON 1--CONGRESS

Revised **Key Terms**:
Add "Politico"

Revised **Textbook Reading Assignment**: pp. 397-408, 417-429, 433-442.

Revised page numbers in the **Answer Key**:

1. p. 400	6. p. 407	11. p. 434
2. p. 400	7. p. 418	12. p. 435
3. pp. 402-403	8. p. 420	13. p. 421
4. p. 403	9. p. 424	14-17. No change
5. p. 405	10. p. 428	

Short Answers:
18. pp. 400-408
19. pp. 400-408

LESSON 3--THE LEGISLATIVE PROCESS

Replace any reference to "Civil Rights Act of 1991" with "Brady Bill of 1993"

Revised **Textbook Reading Assignment**: pp. 429-432.

Revised page numbers in the **Answer Key**:

1. p. 431	4. pp. 430-432	6. p. 430
2. p. 431	5. No change	7-11. No change
3. p. 431		

LESSON 5--THE PRESIDENT AND CONGRESS

Revised **Textbook Reading Assignment**: Chapter 12, pp. 400-402 and pp. 424-429. Chapter 13, pp. 445-446, pp. 449-462, and pp. 464-469.

3. Which of the following is NOT a type of presidential power?
   a. Constitutional power
   b. Statutory power
   c. Inherent power
   d. *De facto* power

4. One way the president has of exerting political power within the party is to
   a. write the party platform.
   b. appoint individuals to government or public jobs.
   c. control what the media print about the party leaders.
   d. determine committee assignments in Congress.

5. Which of the following is NOT a special use of presidential power?
   a. Impeachment power
   b. Emergency power
   c. Executive order
   d. Executive privilege

6. Article I of the U.S. Constitution authorizes the House and Senate to remove the president, vice president, or other civil officers of the United States for treason, bribery, or other high crimes and misdemeanors in a process called
   a. patronage.
   b. executive immunity.
   c. executive order.
   d. impeachment.

7. Under the Constitution, the organization of the executive branch
   a. includes a minimum of four cabinet-level departments.
   b. requires a constitutional amendment to change its structure.
   c. allows for numerous changes in the organization.
   d. cannot be changed more than once by each president.

8. The only formal duty for the vice president provided for in the Constitution is to
   a. preside over the Senate.
   b. represent the president at funerals.
   c. stand in for the president at official functions.
   d. give the opening speech when Congress convenes.

9. One reason the American people expect too much from a president is because the public
   a. expects the president to fulfill campaign promises.
   b. does not understand the five constitutional roles.
   c. is frustrated and wants someone to do something.
   d. bases its opinion of the president on George Washington.

10. Expectations that Jody Powell and Ron Nesson believe the public should have for the president do NOT include the idea that the president will
    a. set a clear direction for the country.
    b. try to keep world peace.
    c. try to reduce the threat of nuclear war.
    d. make sound economic decisions.

11. The urgency of urban and social problems required Lyndon Johnson to emphasize the role of chief
    a. executive.
    b. diplomat.
    c. of state.
    d. legislator.

12. In which of the following ways has television NOT affected the presidency?
    a. It has helped the president focus thoroughly on the issues.
    b. It has made the president more visible.
    c. It has influenced public perceptions of the president.
    d. It has changed the way we elect the president.

13. What one word does Helen Thomas use to describe the presidency?
    a. Intimidating
    b. Powerful
    c. Responsible
    d. Imperial

Short-Answer Question:
14. Do you believe that the power of the presidency is increasing or decreasing? Is this good or bad for the American people? Why?

Answer Key

These are the correct answers with reference to the Learning Objectives, and to the source of the information: the Textbook Focus Points, Schmidt, *et al. American Government and Politics Today* (Schmidt), and the Telelesson Focus Points. Page numbers are also given for the Textbook Focus Points. "KT" indicates questions with Key Terms defined.

Question	Answer	Learning Objective	Textbook Focus Point (page no.)	Telelesson Focus Point
1	C	1	1 (Schmidt, p. 425)	
2	B	2	2 (Schmidt, p. 429)	
3	D	2	3 (Schmidt, pp. 442-443)..KT	
4	B	2	4 (Schmidt, p. 443)	
5	A	3	5 (Schmidt, p. 445)	
6	D	4	6 (Schmidt, p. 447)...........KT	
7	C	5	7 (Schmidt, pp. 448-450)	
8	A	5	8 (Schmidt, p. 454)	
9	B	6		1
10	B	6		2
11	D	3	KT	3
12	A	2		4
13	B	7		5

Short Answer:

14		8	3 (Schmidt, pp. 458-459)	6

GOVERNOR'S MANSION

Lesson 8

The Governor

Overview

The governor of Texas is one of the highest paid governors in the United States. But the person who holds this post is often described as a "first among equals," "the pet rock of Texas politics," or "a well-paid office holder with few powers who must rely on persuasive ability to achieve goals."

The governor is the most visible, easily identifiable, and quickly recognizable of all state officials. Yet the governor of Texas is one of the least powerful governors in the United States.

In Texas, as in most states, the legislature, not the governor, holds the power. In Texas this is especially true, because the legislature dominates the budgetary process; the power of the purse is the power to control.

In other areas, too, the governor has limited constitutional and statutory authority. The most effective governors of Texas succeed as a result of an ability to use their political skills and the power of their personality to persuade legislators and members of the executive branch to act in ways that agree with the governor's thinking.

Learning Objectives

Goal: The goal of this lesson is to describe the office of governor of Texas, in the context of the weak-executive model, and to assess the power the governor has to carry out duties.

Objectives:

1. Discuss the weak-executive model of government in Texas, including the rationale for its adoption and its effect on public perception of the Texas governor.

2. Describe the office of governor of the state of Texas and the interaction of personality with performance.

3. List the executive, legislative, judicial, and informal powers of the governor of Texas.

4. Evaluate the powers of the governor of Texas, emphasizing those powers with greatest significance and greatest limitations.

5. Identify those groups and individuals with ability to influence decisions of the executive branch of Texas government.

Key Terms

Watch for these terms and pay particular attention to what each one means, as you follow the textbook and telelesson.

Weak-executive model	**Martial law**
Chief executive	**Item veto**
Appointive power	**Clemency**
Senatorial courtesy	**Pardon**

Textbook Reading Assignment

Jones, Ericson, Brown, and Trotter. *Practicing Texas Politics,* 8th edition. Chapter 7, "The Executive," pp. 299-360, especially pp. 299-314 and 344-354.

Jones, Ericson, Brown, Trotter, and Lynch. *Practicing Texas Politics – A Brief Survey*, 4th edition. Chapter 7,"The Executive," pp. 189-221, especially pp. 189-202 and 220-221.

Note to the student: You are responsible for only *one* of these reading assignments. It is your responsibility to know which book is used in your class.

Textbook Focus Points

Before you read the textbook assignment, review the following points to help focus your thoughts. After you complete the assignment, write your responses to reinforce what you have learned.

1. What is the weak-executive model? Why does Texas have a weak-executive model and what does it mean for the politics of the Texas executive?

2. What are the qualifications to become governor of Texas? What is the term of office of the governor? How is the salary of the governor of Texas determined? What are reasons for gubernatorial succession, and what is the order of succession? How may a governor be removed from office?

3. What are the governor's executive powers? What limits these powers?

4. What are the governor's legislative powers?

5. What are the governor's judicial powers?

6. What are the governor's informal powers?

7. Which of the governor's powers are most significant?

Telelesson Interviewees

The following individuals will share their expertise in the telelesson.

James Anderson–Department of Political Science, Texas A&M University
George Bayoud–Texas Secretary of State, 1988-1991
William R. Clements–Governor of Texas, 1979-1983, 1987-1991
Charles Elliott, Jr.–Department of Political Science, East Texas State University
William P. Hobby, Jr.–Lieutenant Governor of Texas, 1973-1991
Molly Ivins–Columnist, *Dallas Times Herald*
Sam Kinch–Editor, *Texas Weekly*

Telelesson Focus Points

Before viewing the telelesson, read the following points to help focus your thoughts. After the presentation, write your responses to reinforce these important points.

1. Which two of the governor's powers are most significant?

2. According to Sam Kinch and James Anderson, how does the personality of the individual holding the office of governor affect his or her performance?

3. Why can the governor's power of appointment be significant in its ability to influence state government?

4. What is the difference between what the public expects of the governor of Texas and what the governor can really do?

5. Who really has the ability to influence decisions of the executive branch of Texas government?

Recommended Reading

The following suggestions are not required unless your instructor assigns them. They are listed to let you know where you can find additional information on areas that interest you.

Crawford, Ann Fears, and Jack Keever. *John B. Connally: Portrait in Power*. Austin: Jenkins, 1973.

Reid, Jan. "Ma Ferguson." *Texas Monthly* (September 1986): pp. 128-129.

Sabato, Larry. *Goodbye to Good-time Charlie: The American Governor Transformed*, 2nd edition. Washington, D.C.: 1983.

Getting Involved

These activities are not required unless your instructor assigns them. They offer good suggestions to help you understand and become more involved in the political process.

1. Read news accounts of the reforming of public education in Texas in 1983 and 1984. Pay particular attention to the role of Governor Mark White. Read news accounts of the crisis in funding public education in 1989-1990. Pay particular attention to the role of Governor Bill Clements. Compare the leadership exercised by Governor Clements to that exercised by Governor White. Which do you think used the powers of his office more wisely and effectively?

Self Test

After reading the assignment and watching the telelesson, you should be able to answer these questions. When you have completed the test, turn to the Answer Key to score your answers.

1. The governorship of Texas is identified as a weak-executive model because the governor
   a. has never been elected by an absolute majority of the voters.
   b. exercises little control over the Texas executive branch.
   c. is appointed by the plural executive.
   d. is appointed by a two-thirds majority vote of the Texas legislature.

2. Which of the following is NOT a reason for Texas' weak-executive model?
   a. Dictatorial powers exercised by Governor E.J. Davis
   b. Corruption and scandals which took place under the reconstruction constitution
   c. Public distrust of strong governors
   d. Texas' traditional short ballot

3. To exercise power and leadership, the governor of Texas
   a. relies on constitutional and statutory powers.
   b. gains the trust of the legislature and plural executive.
   c. aligns with power interests such as banking, insurance, and agriculture.
   d. trusts in the position as leader of his or her political party.

4. The constitutional qualifications to become governor of Texas include being
   a. at least thirty years of age.
   b. a resident of Texas for seven years.
   c. a native Texan.
   d. a natural-born citizen of the United States.

5. The salary of the governor of Texas is set by the
   a. Texas Constitution.
   b. Texas legislature.
   c. plural executive.
   d. Governor's Committee on Compensation and Emoluments.

6. The governor of Texas may be removed from office by
   a. impeachment.
   b. impeachment and conviction.
   c. a three-fourths vote of the Texas Supreme Court and Texas Court of Criminal Appeals.
   d. a two-thirds vote of the plural executive and House and Senate Judiciary Committees.

7. The appointive power of the governor of Texas is limited by
   a. senatorial courtesy.
   b. absence of a requirement that the Texas Senate confirm the governor's appointments.
   c. removal power independent of the legislature.
   d. minimum age requirements for the governor's appointees.

8. The governor of Texas appoints
   a. members of the Texas Supreme Court to six-year terms.
   b. individuals to fill vacancies when a U.S. Representative from Texas dies, resigns, or retires.
   c. members of some 200 boards, commissions, and agencies.
   d. the speaker of the Texas House of Representatives.

9. Governors of Texas have power to
   a. remove from office anyone they appointed.
   b. remove from office up to one hundred people per year without the consent of the Texas Senate.
   c. affect the removal of few officials.
   d. recommend that impeachment proceedings be started in the Texas Senate.

10. The temporary rule by the military and suspension of civil authority is
    a. unconstitutional in Texas.
    b. legislative address.
    c. *quo warranto* and part of the governor's law enforcement power.
    d. martial law and part of the governor's military power.

11. Acting alone, the governor of Texas may
    a. impound funds appropriated by the legislature.
    b. veto an individual budget item in an appropriations bill.
    c. transfer funds from one state agency to another.
    d. increase or decrease a state appropriation.

12. The governor's most significant legislative power is the
    a. veto power.
    b. message power.
    c. appointive power.
    d. power to call special sessions.

13. Granting a pardon, commuting a sentence, and granting a thirty-day reprieve are part of the governor's
    a. criminal-justice powers.
    b. executive powers.
    c. legislative powers.
    d. judicial powers.

14. The governor of Texas acts as chief of state when
    a. participating in a public ceremony.
    b. granting a pardon.
    c. appointing a judge.
    d. vetoing a bill.

15. The governor's most significant powers are the power to appoint and power to
    a. remove executive officials from office.
    b. recommend a budget.
    c. influence the legislative process.
    d. work informally towards achieving goals.

16. One of the major factors in determining the effectiveness of a governor in dealing with the legislature and other members of the executive branch is
    a. his or her military service.
    b. the number of years left in his or her term.
    c. size of his or her election victory.
    d. his or her personality.

17. The power of appointment may be significant in efforts to shape the activities of the executive branch, because the governor
    a. often appoints individuals who have similar political and economic philosophies.
    b. recommends individuals for nearly all appointed offices.
    c. retains the authority to dismiss appointed officials who create opposition.
    d. controls each agency's budget.

18. In Texas, a large percentage of the population expects the governor to be able to exercise powers similar to those of the U.S. president,
    a. and, to a large extent, this is true.
    b. and, in fact, the governor has more extensive powers than the president.
    c. and, while the governor has different powers, their ability to control the actions of government is similar.
    d. but, in reality, the governor has few real powers.

19. In Texas, the executive branch of state government is controlled and influenced by
    a. the governor.
    b. individuals with large sums of money.
    c. the plural executive.
    d. lobbyists, the plural executive, the governor, and the state boards and commissions.

Short-Answer Question:
20. List at least three individuals or groups with the ability to significantly influence decisions of the executive branch of Texas government. Briefly describe how these individuals or groups influence the executive branch.

Answer Key

These are the correct answers with reference to the Learning Objectives, and to the source of the information: the Textbook Focus Points, Jones, *et al. Practicing Texas Politics* (Jones) or Jones, *et. al., Practicing Texas Politics — A Brief Survey* (Survey); the Study Guide Overview (Overview); and the Telelesson Focus Points. Page numbers are also given for the Textbook Focus Points. "KT" indicates questions with Key Terms defined.

Question	Answer	Learning Objective	Textbook Focus Point (page no.)	Telelesson Focus Point
1	B	1	1 (Jones, p. 299; Survey, p. 190)...............KT	
2	D	1	1 (Jones, p. 299; Survey, p. 190)	
3	C	1	1 (Jones, p. 301; Survey, p. 192)	
4	A	2	2 (Jones, p. 302; Survey, p. 193)	
5	B	2	2 (Jones, p. 303; Survey, p. 193)	
6	B	2	2 (Jones, p. 304; Survey, p. 194)	
7	A	3	3 (Jones, p. 308; Survey, pp. 196-197)	
8	C	3	3 (Jones, p. 309; Survey, p. 197)	
9	C	3	3 (Jones, pp. 309-310; Survey, p. 198)	
10	D	3	3 (Jones, p. 310; Survey, p. 199)...............KT	
11	B	3	4 (Jones, p. 312; Survey, p. 200)	
12	A	3	4 (Jones, p. 312; Survey, pp. 200-201)	
13	D	3	5 (Jones, p. 313; Survey, pp. 201-202)	
14	A	3	6 (Jones, pp. 313-314; Survey, p. 202)	
15	C	4		1
16	D	2		2
17	A	4		3
18	D	1		4
19	D	5		5

Short Answer:

20		5		5

Lesson 9

The Bureaucracy

Overview

What comes to your mind when you hear the terms "bureaucracy" or "red tape"? When we asked this question, most people answered with such terms as "big," "wasteful," "inefficient," and "frustrated"—just to name a few. If you remember some of the candidates' promises from the last several presidential campaigns, you probably recall that most candidates promised to clean up the bureaucracy. These were not idle promises; their intentions were good. But were they able to achieve any results?

This lesson looks at the bureaucracy with an unbiased eye and identifies its role in our governmental process. We define bureaucracy, investigate its functions, and see how well it performs these functions.

Then we turn our attention to how the National Park Service, part of the U.S. Department of Interior, fought the massive forest fires that burned across the western states in 1988 by enforcing the policies that had been developed for such occasions. Due to public outcry, pressure on politicians, and media attention, these policies were slowly changed—proving that federal agencies do respond to criticism.

Next, we consider the Internal Revenue Service, without doubt one of the most pervasive—some say invasive—of all federal agencies, as it affects virtually everyone who lives in the United States. The IRS exemplifies all the characteristics of a bureaucracy, both good and bad. But it too can change, as it did in 1988 after Congress passed the "Taxpayers' Bill of Rights."

The U.S. bureaucracy has become so large and affects so many areas of our lives that it has been called "the fourth branch of government." It is massive, but we also ask it to perform herculean tasks—such as delivering the mail all across the United States in every kind of climatic condition for under 50 cents. Given the role that government plays in our lives, we need to understand how and why the bureaucracy works as it does. Then, when changes are necessary, we will know how and where to begin!

Learning Objectives

Goal: The purpose of "The Bureaucracy" is to assess the extent to which the bureaucracy responds to our needs, and to recognize when and how the bureaucracy should be held accountable or changed.

Objectives:

1. Outline strategies used by Congress and the president to control our bureaucracies, often called the "permanent government."

2. Define "bureaucracy" and list some of the activities it does well and some, not so well.

3. Describe how the organization and staffing of the federal bureaucracy has evolved, emphasizing its phenomenal growth.

4. Analyze recent attempts to reform the federal bureaucracy and make it more accountable.

5. Explain the roles that bureaucrats play as politicians, policymakers, and nonpolitical public servants.

6. List some ways that individuals can deal effectively with the federal bureaucracy.

7. Illustrate the typical responsiveness of the bureaucracy, using the examples of the National Park Service fighting forest fires in 1988 and the Internal Revenue Service participating in tax reform.

Key Terms

Watch for these terms and pay particular attention to what each one means, as you follow the textbook and telelesson.

Bureaucracy

Cabinet departments

Independent executive agency

Independent regulatory agency

Government corporation

Spoils system

Merit system

Pendleton Act

Civil Service Commission

Hatch Act

Government in the
  Sunshine Act

Sunset legislation

Whistle-blower

Iron triangle

Textbook Reading Assignment

Schmidt, Shelley, and Bardes. *American Government and Politics Today*, 1993-94 edition. Chapter 14, "The Bureaucracy," pp. 463-491.

Textbook Focus Points

Before you read the textbook assignment, review the following points to help focus your thoughts. After you complete the assignment, write out your responses to reinforce what you have learned.

1. How successful have presidents been in controlling or changing the federal bureaucracy?

2. What is a bureaucracy, and what are some of its characteristics?

3. How is the federal bureaucracy organized?

4. How has the staffing of the federal bureaucracy evolved?

5. What are some recent attempts to reform the federal bureaucracy?

6. How do bureaucrats play the roles of politicians and policymakers, when they are supposed to be nonpolitical?

7. How does Congress try to control the federal bureaucracy?

Telelesson Interviewees

The following individuals share their expertise in the telelesson:

Gary A. Booth–Director, Dallas District, Internal Revenue Service
Brad Leonard–Acting Director, Office of Program Analysis, U.S. Department of Interior
Peter Woll–Professor of Political Science, Brandeis University
Sherman Wyman–Professor, Institute of Urban Studies, University of Texas, Arlington

Telelesson Focus Points

Before viewing the telelesson, read over the following points to help focus your thoughts. After the presentation, write out your responses to help you remember these important points.

1. What is the estimated size of the federal bureaucracy, and why has it grown so?

2. What types of activities does the bureaucracy do well and not so well?

3. How can individuals deal effectively with the federal bureaucracy?

4. Why is the bureaucracy often called the "permanent government," and how does this permanency affect the operation of government?

5. How does the example of the National Park Service fighting forest fires in 1988 illustrate the way bureaucracies operate?

6. How does the Internal Revenue Service typify a classic bureaucracy, and what has been done to make it more responsive?

7. To whom is the bureaucracy accountable, and when and by whom should it be called to account for its actions?

Recommended Reading

The following suggestions are not required unless your instructor assigns them. They are listed to let you know where you can find additional information on areas which interest you.

Alter, Jonathan. "The Powers that Stay" in Peter Woll's *Behind the Scenes in American Government: Personalities and Politics*, 6th edition. Boston: Little, Brown and Company, 1987, pp. 354-364.

"Congress Has Leveled the Playing Field for Contests with the Tax Man." *U.S. News & World Report* 106 (March 27, 1989): p.79.

Woll, Peter. "Constitutional Democracy and Bureaucratic Power" in *Public Administration and Policy*. Boston: Little, Brown and Company, 1966, pp. 1-14.

"Your Rights as a Taxpayer." *Consumers Research Magazine* 72 (March 1989): pp. 20-24.

Getting Involved

These activities are not required unless your instructor assigns them. But they offer good suggestions to help you understand and become more involved in the political process.

1. Visit your local post office and ask the officials to show you how a letter gets from your home mail box to its final destination. If you live in a large city, you might like to go to both your own branch and the main post office, to see the total picture. Ask the people with whom you talk to estimate how much a private company would charge to deliver the same letter.

2. Note the "Getting Involved" section in your textbook at the end of Chapter 14.

3. Most of us have to file an income tax report each year. To learn how your report is processed, contact a local Internal Revenue Service office and ask for an official to explain to you the normal procedure for processing a claim.

Self Test

After reading the assignment and watching the telelesson, you should be able to answer these questions. When you have completed the test, turn to the Answer Key to score your answers.

1. Presidential attempts to affect significantly the structure and operation of the federal bureaucracy are
   a. very successful.
   b. a result of hard work that is now beginning to pay off.
   c. generally unsuccessful.
   d. worthwhile when Congress has been controlled by Democrats.

2. Bureaucracy is the name given to any
   a. large branch of a government that has power to make laws.
   b. organization that has major problems when attempting to accomplish its goals.
   c. group of people who work together to enforce policies in a way that prevents quick results.
   d. large organization that is structured hierarchically and is supposed to carry out specific functions.

3. Which one of the following is NOT a major type of bureaucratic structure?
   a. Cabinet departments
   b. Copyright Royalty Tribunal
   c. Independent executive agencies
   d. Independent regulatory agencies

4. The president is able to make political appointments to most of the top jobs in the federal bureaucracy, but the rest of the individuals who work for the national government got their jobs through
   a. the merit system of the civil service department.
   b. appointment based on membership in the natural aristocracy.
   c. helping get the president elected and relying on the spoils system.
   d. passing a battery of tests and applying through Congress.

5. Which of the following is NOT a recent attempt at reforming the federal bureaucracy?
   a. Privatization
   b. Sunshine and sunset laws
   c. Protection for whistle-blowers
   d. Department of Veteran Affairs

6. A realistic view of the role of the bureaucracy in policymaking is that agencies and departments of government
   a. play a neutral role in making policy.
   b. provide only relevant information to the policymakers.
   c. administer without attempting to influence policies.
   d. play an important role in making policy.

7. The ultimate check that Congress has over the bureaucracy is the ability to
   a. hire and fire members of boards and commissions.
   b. write legislation in terms so vague that the bureaucracy will not be able to interpret the meaning.
   c. withhold appropriations of money to the bureaucracy.
   d. influence the president to take action against a bureaucrat.

8. Which of the following reasons does NOT account for the continued growth of the federal bureaucracy?
   a. New technological advancements
   b. New policies set by new presidents
   c. New laws enacted by Congress
   d. Increases in the nation's population

9. According to Sherman Wyman, which of the following activities does a bureaucracy NOT do well?
   a. Provide a valuable financial resource
   b. Provide a water supply
   c. Provide a fascinating career arena
   d. Provide police and fire protection

10. Sherman Wyman recommends that individuals deal with the bureaucracy by
   a. being dogmatic in order not to give the bureaucracy an opportunity to respond.
   b. researching a request much as you would if applying for a federal grant.
   c. defending your position so that you cannot be accused of being negligent.
   d. approaching the bureaucracy much as you would approach a friend or any other group of people.

11. Presidents, members of Congress, and some federal judges come and go, but most of the bureaucrats remain on the job–causing the bureaucracy to be referred to as the
   a. government in the sunshine.
   b. permanent government.
   c. government corporation.
   d. seniority system.

12. The actions of the National Park Service during the 1988 forest fires typify the bureaucracy, because the
   a. head of the agency inspected the area before action was taken.
   b. new fire fighters hired to fight the fires were terminated.
   c. Park Service was very slow to change its policies.
   d. strategies were carefully mapped out with input from many agencies.

13. Which of the following traits of the Internal Revenue Services does NOT typify the classic traits of a bureaucracy?
   a. Large size
   b. Complex organization
   c. Strict compliance to rules
   d. Adaptable to change

14. Bureaucratic experts like Peter Woll believe the bureaucracy should be accountable to the
    a. public through our elected officials.
    b. media through their power to report the news.
    c. president as the chief executive.
    d. cabinet directors who head the various agencies.

Short-Answer Question:
15. If you were an incoming president, what reforms would you recommend for the federal bureaucracy and how would you implement them?

Answer Key

These are the correct answers with reference to the Learning Objectives, and to the source of the information: the Textbook Focus Points, Schmidt, *et al. American Government and Politics Today* (Schmidt), and the Telelesson Focus Points. Page numbers are also given for the Textbook Focus Points. "KT" indicates questions with Key Terms defined.

Question	Answer	Learning Objective	Textbook Focus Point (page no.)	Telelesson Focus Point
1	C	1	1 (Schmidt, p. 465)	
2	D	2	2 (Schmidt, p. 465)	KT
3	B	3	3 (Schmidt, p. 469)	
4	A	3	4 (Schmidt, p. 475)	
5	D	4	5 (Schmidt, p. 481)	
6	D	5	6 (Schmidt, p. 485)	
7	C	1	7 (Schmidt, p. 486)	
8	A	3		1
9	A	2		2
10	D	6		3
11	B	1		4
12	C	7		5
13	D	7		6
14	A	4		7

Short Answer:

15		4		7

The Plural Executive

Overview

Under the reconstruction constitution of 1869, the governor appointed judges and most executive officers. While Governor E.J. Davis is generally regarded as an honest politician, his appointees were accused of malfeasance, bribery, and corruption. When Texans had the opportunity to draft a new constitution in 1876, they chose to limit executive power and disperse it through several elected officials, called the "plural executive."

Advocates of the "plural executive" concept believe it limits the power of executive officials and makes these officers more accountable to the public. Opponents assert that the plural executive is inefficient and does not promote good government, and that the public is ill-equipped to choose among candidates for these offices.

Texans elect seven of the eight people who comprise the plural executive: the governor, lieutenant governor, attorney general, comptroller of public accounts, state treasurer, commissioner of the general land office, and commissioner of agriculture. The governor appoints the eighth person, the secretary of state.

The governor's role is considered in another lesson. The lieutenant governor officially performs as an executive only when the governor is absent from the state or on succession to the governorship. The other six officials— attorney general, comptroller of public accounts, state treasurer, commissioner of the general land office, commissioner of agriculture, and secretary of state—form the basis for this examination of the plural executive.

In this lesson the duties and responsibilities of each member of the plural executive are described briefly, and the general land office is studied in some detail. L. Tucker Gibson, a political scientist at Trinity University, offers his evaluation of the efficiency and effectiveness of the plural executive. The Austin Bureau chief for the *Houston Chronicle*, Clay Robison, examines how and to whom the plural executive is accountable.

The lesson asserts that the business of Texas government is conducted under the plural executive, but a less fragmented form of government might be more efficient.

Learning Objectives

Goal: The purpose of this lesson is to evaluate the effectiveness of the plural executive as it operates in Texas.

Objectives:

1. Explain the concept of "plural executive," including why it was adopted in Texas, why it is considered weak, and to whom it is accountable.

2. Evaluate the potential for eliminating the plural executive in Texas, citing advantages and disadvantages of the system.

3. Identify the officials who compose the plural executive in Texas, and assess the relative power of each.

4. List the term of office, the constitutional qualifications for holding office, and the method of selection for each member of the plural executive in Texas.

5. Describe the duties of the members of the plural executive in Texas.

Key Term

Watch for this term and pay particular attention to what it means, as you follow the textbook and telelesson.

Weak executive

Textbook Reading Assignment

Jones, Ericson, Brown, and Trotter. *Practicing Texas Politics,* 8th edition. Chapter 7, "The Executive," pp. 299- 360, especially pp. 314-319.

Jones, Ericson, Brown, Trotter, and Lynch. *Practicing Texas Politics – A Brief Survey*, 4th edition. Chapter 7, "The Executive," pp. 189-221, especially pp. 202-206.

Note to students: You are responsible for only *one* of these reading assignments. It is your responsibility to know which book is used in your class.

Textbook Focus Points

Before you read the textbook assignment, review the following points to help focus your thoughts. After you complete the assignment, write your responses to reinforce what you have learned.

1. What officials make up the plural executive? How are they selected and what are their terms of office? How does the plural executive contribute to the weak-executive structure?

2. What are the constitutional qualifications and duties of the lieutenant governor, attorney general, commissioner of the general land office, commissioner of agriculture, comptroller of public accounts, state treasurer, and secretary of state?

3. What is the relative power of each office holder?

Telelesson Interviewees

The following individuals will share their expertise in the telelesson:

George Bayoud–Former Texas Secretary of State
L. Tucker Gibson–Department of Political Science, Trinity University
William P. Hobby, Jr.–Former Lieutenant Governor of Texas
Sam Kinch–Editor, *Texas Weekly*
Jim Mattox–Former Attorney General of Texas
Gary Mauro–Commissioner of the General Land Office
Ann Richards–Governor and former State Treasurer
Clay Robison–Austin Bureau Chief, *Houston Chronicle*

Telelesson Focus Points

Before viewing the telelesson, read over the following points to help focus your thoughts. After the presentation, write out your responses to help you remember these important points.

1. Why does Texas have a plural executive? What does it do well and not so well?

2. According to Ann Richards, what is the responsibility of the state treasurer?

3. According to Jim Mattox, what are the duties of the attorney general?

4. According to Gary Mauro, what are the duties of the commissioner of the general land office?

5. Does the plural executive provide Texas with efficient government? What is the likelihood of significant reform?

6. To whom is the plural executive accountable?

Recommended Reading

The following suggestions are not required unless your instructor assigns them. They are listed to let you know where you can find additional information on areas which interest you.

De Marco, Susan. "Home-Grown Agriculture: The Hightower Revolution in Texas." *Southern Exposure* nos. 5-6 (1986): pp. 65-70.

Dickson, James D. *Law and Politics: The Office of Attorney General in Texas.* Austin: Sterling Swift, 1976.

Guide to Texas State Agencies, 7th ed. Austin: LBJ School of Public Affairs, UT Austin, 1992.

The Land Commissioners of Texas. Austin: Texas General Land Office. 1986.

McNeeley, Dave. "Prophet of the Purse Strings." *D* (July 1986): pp. 36, 38-40.

Getting Involved

This activity is not required unless your instructor assigns it. But it offers good suggestions to help you understand and become more involved in the political process.

In a Texas newspaper, find an editorial that relates to officials or agencies of the plural executive. Write a letter to the editor explaining why you agree or disagree with that editorial.

Self Test

After reading the assignment and watching the telelesson, you should be able to answer these questions. When you have completed the test, turn to the Answer Key to score your answers.

1. In Texas, the only member of the plural executive appointed to office is the
   a. lieutenant governor.
   b. state treasurer.
   c. commissioner of agriculture.
   d. secretary of state.

2. In Texas, the plural executive contributes to a weak-executive structure by dividing power among officials who are
   a. appointed to the governor's cabinet.
   b. elected to the governor's cabinet.
   c. basically independent of the control of the governor.
   d. chairpersons of Texas' 200 boards, commissions, and agencies.

3. In Texas, legislative duties are the most important responsibility of the
   a. lieutenant governor.
   b. attorney general.
   c. secretary of state.
   d. state treasurer.

4. The individual responsible for providing advisory opinions to state and local authorities throughout Texas is the
   a. lieutenant governor.
   b. attorney general.
   c. governor's chief counsel.
   d. secretary of state.

5. In Texas, the individual principally responsible for administering deposits of state funds is the
   a. secretary of state.
   b. chair, Texas Banking Commission.
   c. comptroller of public accounts.
   d. state treasurer.

6. According to your textbook, the two most powerful officials in Texas government are the lieutenant governor and the
   a. attorney general.
   b. secretary of state.
   c. governor.
   d. commissioner of the general land office.

7. The Texas Constitution provides for a plural executive because the framers of the constitution feared placing too much power in the hands of any one individual, a legacy from
   a. cattle barons of west Texas.
   b. Mexican rule.
   c. reconstruction.
   d. Spanish colonial governors.

8. In Texas, the primary responsibility of the state treasurer is
   a. safety of the state's money.
   b. high return on investment.
   c. swift processing of state deposits and negotiable warrants.
   d. service to the state bond review committee.

9. In Texas, the primary area of responsibility for the attorney general is to
   a. appeal death penalty cases.
   b. serve as the state's chief prosecuting attorney.
   c. serve as the state's chief civil attorney.
   d. appeal all criminal cases from district court to the court of criminal appeals.

10. Traditionally, a major responsibility of the general land office was to
    a. acquire as much land as possible for Texas.
    b. give away Texas' public lands.
    c. sell public land for as much money as possible.
    d. auction rights to natural resources found on public lands.

11. In recent years, the commissioner of the general land office has undertaken responsibilities for certain environmental concerns, including
    a. recycling tires as an additive to asphalt on roads.
    b. an "adopt a polluter" program.
    c. fining petroleum producers who pollute the state's streams and rivers.
    d. using compressed natural gas as a motor fuel.

12. According to experts in the video, significant reform in the plural executive is
    a. just around the corner.
    b. likely within the next five years.
    c. likely when the Constitution of 2001 comes into being.
    d. unlikely.

13. The plural executive is primarily accountable to the
    a. governor.
    b. courts.
    c. voters.
    d. lieutenant governor.

Short-Answer Question:
14. What are the advantages and disadvantages of the plural executive government in Texas?

Answer Key

These are the correct answers with reference to the Learning Objectives, and to the source of the information: the Textbook Focus Points, Jones, *et al. Practicing Texas Politics* (Jones) or Jones, *et. al., Practicing Texas Politics — A Brief Survey* (Survey); the Study Guide Overview (Overview); and the Telelesson Focus Points. Page numbers are also given for the Textbook Focus Points. "KT" indicates questions with Key Terms defined.

Question	Answer	Learning Objective	Textbook Focus Point (page no.)	Telelesson Focus Point
1	D	4	1 (Jones, pp. 314, 318-319; Survey, pp. 202, 205-206)	
2	C	1	1 (Jones, p. 314; Survey, p. 202)	
3	A	5	2 (Jones, p. 314; Survey, p. 203)	
4	B	5	2 (Jones, p. 315; Survey, p. 203)	
5	D	5	2 (Jones, p. 317-318; Survey, p. 205)	
6	C	3	3 (Jones, pp. 314-319; Survey, pp. 203-206)	
7	C	1		1
8	A	5		2
9	C	5		3
10	B	5		4
11	D	5		4
12	D	2		5
13	C	1		6

Short Answer:

14		2		5

SOCIAL SECURITY
XXX-XX-XXXX
THIS NUMBER HAS BEEN ESTABLISHED FOR
JOHN DOE
SIGNATURE

Lesson 11

Domestic Policy

Overview

This lesson brings together every component of the governmental process that we have studied so far: the constitutional basis, the participation of the people through interest groups and political parties, the process of electing a president and members of Congress, the political institutions of Congress and the presidency, the legislative process, and the federal bureaucracy. All of these elements must cooperate to produce a product, such as domestic policy or foreign policy.

In looking at the legislative process, we followed the steps to pass a bill and sign it into law. In our study of the bureaucracy, we found out how a law is turned into policy. Now we define domestic policy: all of the national laws and actions that affect life within the nation's borders. Since the president and Congress are responsible for making domestic policy, we examine the basic steps in developing such a policy: building, formulating, adopting, implementing, and evaluating an agenda.

Next, we find out how various kinds of domestic policy are implemented. To accomplish this, we look at an agency that affects almost every one of us, either through the taxes we pay to it or the benefits we receive from it: the Social Security Administration. In the process we see the concept and costs of trade-offs in action.

With 535 members of Congress representing the 50 states, everybody wants something; there is an infinite number of requests for a finite amount of resources. This situation produces another kind of trade-off: We increase the amount of funds spent on welfare but reduce what is spent on the environment; we increase military spending but reduce aid to education. The textbook calls this an "action-reaction syndrome."

Basically, we must realize that setting domestic policy is an ongoing process, and one that is constantly open to change. In addition, we are continually faced with numerous problems in search of solutions; there rarely is consensus on how these problems should be solved. Consequently, we need to voice our concerns and become actively involved in affecting the decision-making process. For only then will we have a say in the policies that affect us.

Learning Objectives

Goal: The purpose of "Domestic Policy" is to illustrate how the legislative and executive branches produce domestic policy, which affects us all.

Objectives:

1. Explain the policy-making process from the time a nation or state becomes aware of a problem requiring government attention, through the final implementation and enforcement of action on it by the bureaucracy.

2. Show how the way that domestic policy is carried out affects individuals, specifically the lack of comprehensive health-care, the increase of poverty and homelessness, environmental policy, and the concern for public safety and crime.

3. Describe processes used by Congress to determine domestic priorities and how congressional oversight affects the setting of the national agenda.

4. Illustrate the implementation of domestic policy, citing the 1987 funding package for the Department of Transportation and resolution of the social security crisis of the early 1980s as examples.

---

resolution of the social security crisis of the early 1980s as examples.

Key Terms

Watch for these terms and pay particular attention to what each one means, as you follow the textbook and telelesson.

Policy trade-offs	**National agenda (TV)**
Social Security	**Domestic policy (TV)**
Income transfer	

Textbook Reading Assignment

Schmidt, Shelley, and Bardes. *American Government and Politics Today,* 1993-94 edition. Chapter 16, "Politics of Economic Policy Making," pp. 529-537, 554, and Chapter 17, "Domestic Policy," pp. 557-591.

Textbook Focus Points

Before you read the textbook assignment, review the following points to help focus your thoughts. After you complete the assignment, write out your responses to reinforce what you have learned.

1. How does a nation or state become aware of a problem that governments need to address, and how is a solution found?

2. How does the American government address the problems of health-care, poverty, and homelessness?

3. How has the government reacted to environmental problems?

4. How does the government handle the problems of public safety and crime in America?

5. How does the American government combat the drug problem?

Telelesson Interviewees

The following individuals will share their expertise in the telelesson:

Thomas S. Foley–Democrat; U.S. Representative, State of Washington; Speaker of the House

William Gray–Democrat; U.S. Representative, Pennsylvania; House Majority Whip

Don P. Watson–Regional Administrator, Southwest Region, Federal Aviation Administration

Aaron Wildavsky–Professor of Political Science and Public Policy, University of California, Berkley

Telelesson Focus Points

Before viewing the telelesson, read over the following points to help focus your thoughts. After the presentation, write out your responses to help you remember these important points.

1. What are "domestic policy" and "national agenda," and how are they determined?

2. Explain how the 1987 funding package for the Department of Transportation was developed.

3. According to Aaron Wildavsky, how is American domestic policy made and what changes are needed in the process?

4. What was the social security crisis in the early 1980s, and how was it resolved?

5. According to William Gray, what are the consequences of social security benefits being "untouchable"?

6. How does Tom Foley say Congress determines domestic priorities?

7. How does congressional oversight affect domestic policy?

Recommended Reading

The following suggestions are not required unless your instructor assigns them. But they are listed to let you know where you can find additional information on areas which interest you.

Anderson, Harry. "The Social Security Crisis." *Newsweek* 101 (January 24, 1983): pp. 18-23+.

Harrington, Michael. *The New American Poverty.* New York: Penguin Books, 1985.

Hildreth, James M. "Social Security Rescue–What It Means to You." *U.S. News & World Report* 94 (April 4, 1983): pp. 23-25.

Peterson, Peter G. "Can Social Security Be Saved?" *Reader's Digest* 122 (March 1983): pp. 49-54.

Wohl, Burton. *China Syndrome.* New York: Bantam Books, 1979.

Getting Involved

These activities are not required unless your instructor assigns them. But they offer good suggestions to help you understand and become more involved in the political process.

1. Note the "Getting Involved" section of your textbook at the end of Chapter 16 and Chapter 17.

2. Contact a federal agency in your area, such as the Social Security Administration or the Food and Drug Administration, to learn what domestic-policy programs are being implemented by that agency. Find out how that agency affects you.

Self Test

After reading the assignment and watching the telelesson, you should be able to answer these questions. When you have completed the test, turn to the Answer Key to score your answers.

1. The concept of agenda adoption refers to the
   a. specific strategy being selected from among the various proposals discussed.
   b. final compromise between Congress and the executive branch.
   c. policy disputes mediated by the Office of Management and Budget.
   d. specific plan of action from the Congressional Budget Office.

2. One factor that effects the changing demographics of our population is
   a. Ellis Island is now closed to immigrants.
   b. U.S. Immigration Service has been dismantled.
   c. the U.S. population is getting older.
   d. the population continues to move to the suburbs.

3. Which of the following groups is NOT included among the "new poor"?
   a. Single-parent families
   b. Rainbow coalition
   c. Youth
   d. Single elderly people

---

4. The National Environmental Policy Act of 1969 did NOT
   a. establish the Council for Environmental Quality.
   b. mandate that an environmental impact statement be prepared for every action affecting the quality of the environment.
   c. require a feasibility study accompany each request for federal funds for environmental projects.
   d. give citizens a weapon against the government for unnecessary & inappropriate use of resources.

5. What most Americans are worried about is
   a. violent crime.
   b. catastrophic events.
   c. nuclear attack.
   d. financial collapse.

6. What is considered the major source of America's public safety crisis?
   a. Traffic violations
   b. Gangs
   c. Illegal drugs
   d. Unregulated gun control

7. Those things that the national government does and does not do to make our society a better place to live make up this nation's
   a. agenda.
   b. domestic policy.
   c. public assistance.
   d. social insurance.

8. In the formulation of the Department of Transportation funding package, questions related to
   a. what the total amount would be for the department to plan its projects.
   b. which section of the budget the package would be placed.
   c. who would administer the funds: the national government or the states.
   d. which specific items would be cut to help reduce the federal deficit.

9. According to Aaron Wildavsky, U.S. domestic policy is made by the
   a. special interest groups who lobby Congress.
   b. president because he represents the interests of the entire nation.
   c. military because it doesn't want funds removed from foreign policy.
   d. people who are elected for that purpose.

10. Because people were living longer and receiving benefits for a longer period of time, and because benefits were increased without raising taxes, the social security system in the early 1980s was almost
    a. bankrupt.
    b. solvent.
    c. volatile.
    d. prosperous.

11. According to William Gray, the untouchability of social security benefits takes a significant chunk out of the national budget, which means that deficit reduction must
    a. be addressed before finalizing the budget.
    b. be taken out of the military budget.
    c. come out of other programs.
    d. become a priority item on the national agenda.

12. Which of the following is NOT one of the questions that Tom Foley says must be answered in order for Congress to set priorities and reach a consensus on the budget resolution?
    a. Where should the country go?
    b. Who should implement the country's goals?
    c. How many resources should be applied to reach goals?
    d. What kinds of resources should be applied to reach goals?

Short-Answer Question:
13. How does congressional oversight affect domestic policy?

Answer Key

These are the correct answers with reference to the Learning Objectives, and to the source of the information: the Textbook Focus Points, Schmidt, *et al. American Government and Politics Today* (Schmidt), and the Telelesson Focus Points. Page numbers are also given for the Textbook Focus Points. "KT" indicates questions with Key Terms defined.

Question	Answer	Learning Objective	Textbook Focus Point (page no.)	Telelesson Focus Point
1	A	1	1 (Schmidt, p. 532)	
2	C	2	2 (Schmidt, p. 560)	
3	B	2	2 (Schmidt, p. 567)	
4	C	2	3 (Schmidt, pp. 574-575)	
5	A	2	4 (Schmidt, p. 583)	
6	C	2	5 (Schmidt, p. 584)	
7	B	3		KT ... 1
8	D	4		2
9	D	3		KT ... 3
10	A	4		4
11	C	4		5
12	B	3		6

Short Answer:

13		4	1 (Schmidt, pp. 531-533) .. KT	7

TEXAS EMPLOYMENT
COMMISSION

TEXAS HIGHWAY DEPARTMENT
DISTRICT 18

Lesson 12

Bureaucracy of Texas Government

Overview

The executive branch of Texas government is much larger than the governor. It also includes all of the agencies of state government that administer or carry out the laws and policies set by the legislative branch and by other parts of the executive branch of government. This body of nonelected officials is called the bureaucracy. The people who work in these bureaucratic agencies are known as bureaucrats.

Most of us need little introduction to the Texas bureaucracy, because we come in contact with its activities every time we show our driver's license, pay a sales tax, or ride on a highway built and maintained with state funds. We also see the bureaucracy at work if we file for unemployment compensation or a title for a motor vehicle.

The bureaucracy of Texas government includes the staffs of duly elected officials such as the governor, lieutenant governor, attorney general, comptroller of public accounts, and commissioner of agriculture, as well as the staffs of approximately two hundred appointed boards, commissions, and agencies. Legislators, governors and other elected officials may come and go, but the bureaucracy remains as the permanent part of government which provides continuity and expertise.

Consequently, bureaucracy is hierarchical—organized by rank—and adheres to encyclopedic sets of rules and regulations. This adherence to regulations is a major criticism of bureaucracies, but it also is what makes them perform effectively. The fact that a bureaucracy follows specific rules, instead of operating creatively, means that each individual who comes into contact with the bureaucracy is treated the same. Further, the state bureaucracy must be responsible to the legislature, to the chief executive, and, most of all, to the people of Texas.

The telelesson examines the three types of bureaucratic units found in Texas: those with a single elected administrator, those with a single appointed administrator, and those boards and commissions with more than one head. We then explore the functions of the Texas bureaucracy: education, service, regulation, licensing, and promotion.

The Texas Department of Highways and Public Transportation offers a good example of a bureaucratic agency which is well funded, well known and performs well. Its function is best seen by viewing its products: over 275,000 miles of highways, some 30,000 bridges, at least 800 picnic areas, and hundreds of roadside rest areas, plus a myriad of services including tourist information, vehicle titles and registration, outside advertising, junkyard control, and highway and vehicle safety programs.

Bureaucracies are always being criticized for being slow to respond, impersonal, and filled with red tape. In fact, the Texas bureaucracy often is criticized by the people of Texas and castigated by the media as a bumbling band of beings who do very little. This lesson attacks that belief by illustrating how the Texas bureaucracy does many things very well. It also shows how the Texas bureaucracy is accountable to the legislature and the governor, and thus to the people of Texas, through the budgetary process and periodic sunset review.

Learning Objectives

Goal: The purpose of this lesson is to illustrate the functions of the bureaucracy in Texas in implementing legislation and serving the needs of citizens.

Objectives:

1. Describe the bureaucracy as it functions in the state of Texas, including policy activities and its success in fulfilling its role.

2. Discuss the role of the bureaucracy in implementing legislation associated with higher education in Texas.

3. Explain the function of the bureaucracy in providing health and human services to citizens of Texas, especially in reacting to the AIDS issue.

4. Review the missions of agencies in the Texas bureaucracy that deal with economic and transportation needs of the state.

5. Assess the problems of bureaucratic proliferation in Texas, with references to solutions.

Key Terms

Watch for these terms and pay particular attention to what each one means, as you follow the textbook and telelesson.

Board-commission system   **Licensing boards**
Intrastate commerce   **Sunset Advisory Commission**

Textbook Reading Assignment

Jones, Ericson, Brown, and Trotter. *Practicing Texas Politics,* 8th edition. Chapter 7, "The Executive," pp. 299-360, especially pp. 319-360.

Jones, Ericson, Brown, Trotter, and Lynch. *Practicing Texas Politics - A Brief Survey,* 4th edition. Chapter 7, "The Executive," pp. 189-221, especially pp. 206-221.

Note to students: You are responsible for only *one* of these reading assignments. It is your responsibility to know which book is used in your class.

Textbook Focus Points

1. Who controls the Texas government? What is the size of the bureaucracy?

2. What group controls higher education in Texas? What was the purpose of the Select Committee on Higher Education?

3. What issues are covered under the term "human services"? What agencies and what programs come under "human services"?

4. What agencies are involved with aging, health, and employment? What are some of their programs?

5. What agencies are involved with economic regulation? Describe the area of responsibility and governing board of each agency. What is the function of licensing boards? What is the responsibility and composition of the Texas Department of Commerce?

6. What is the cause and resultant problem of bureaucratic proliferation? What is the function of the Sunset Advisory Commission?

7. What has been Texas' response to the AIDS issue?

Interviewees

Alvin Granoff–Member, Texas House of Representatives, Dallas
James Kaster–Chair, Texas Employment Commission
David McNeeley–Journalist, *Austin American Statesman*
Jim Moore–Journalist, KPRC-TV, Houston, Texas
Charldean Newell–Department of Political Science, University of North Texas
Arnold Oliver–Chief Engineer, Texas Department of Highways and Public Transportation

Telelesson Focus Points

Before viewing the telelesson, read the following points to help focus your thoughts. After the presentation, write your responses to help you remember these important points.

1. What are the five basic policy activities of the Texas bureaucracy?

2. According to Professor Charldean Newell, what does the Texas bureaucracy do and how well does it do it?

3. What is the mission of the Texas Department of Highways and Public Transportation?

4. What is the "sunset review" process, and how does it hold agencies accountable to the legislature?

Recommended Reading

The following suggestions are not required unless your instructor assigns them. They are listed to let you know where you can find additional information about areas which interest you.

Davis, Mary Alice. *Disciplining the Doctors: Medical Regulation in Texas.* Austin: House Research Organization, 1987.

Prindle, David F. *Petroleum Politics and the Texas Railroad Commission.* Austin: University of Texas Press, 1981.

Self Test

After reading the assignment and watching the telelesson, you should be able to answer these questions. When you have completed the test, turn to the Answer Key to score your answers.

1. In reference to state government in Texas, questions such as "Who's in charge here?" are best answered by an examination of the
   a. governor of Texas.
   b. Texas bureaucracy.
   c. Sunset Advisory Commission.
   d. Legislative Research Organization.

2. The largest employer in Texas is
   a. Texas Instruments.
   b. Exxon corporation.
   c. state government.
   d. federal government.

3. The group which loosely oversees higher education in Texas is the
   a. Texas Higher Education Coordinating Board.
   b. State Board of Higher Education.
   c. State Board of Colleges and Universities.
   d. Texas State Board of Education.

4. Issues involving suffering from poverty, illness, and joblessness can be broadly classified as issues involving
   a. ethnic groups.
   b. migrant groups.
   c. welfare services.
   d. human services.

5. The agency with primary responsibility for providing most human services in Texas is the Texas Department of
   a. Human Services.
   b. Welfare.
   c. Public Health and Welfare.
   d. Texas Employment Commission.

6. The agency responsible for developing and strengthening public and private services for Texas' elderly population is the Texas Department
   a. of Human Services.
   b. of Health.
   c. of Aging.
   d. of Health and Human Services.

7. Administering the federally funded Medicare program, evaluating health maintenance organizations, and licensing over 500 hospitals is the responsibility of the Texas Department
   a. of Human Services.
   b. of Health.
   c. of Aging.
   d. of Health and Human Services.

8. Texas policymakers must make difficult decisions within an ever-changing political context due to
   a. a diverse economy.
   b. the federal government's demands.
   c. complex economic problems.
   d. "a" and "c" are correct.

9. The regulation of intrastate commerce is the primary responsibility of the Texas
   a. Interstate Commerce Commission.
   b. Intrastate Commerce Commission.
   c. Business Regulation Commission.
   d. Railroad Commission.

10. The Texas Railroad Commission (Jones, 8th ed.)
    a. regulates all interstate commerce.
    b. establishes electric rates.
    c. oversees the airline industry.
    d. does not regulate railroads.

11. The governor's influence over licensing commissions is pervasive because the governor
    a. establishes standards for professional conduct.
    b. appoints virtually all members of licensing boards.
    c. controls the budgets of these agencies.
    d. possesses absolute power to remove members of licensing boards.

12. The group which studies each state agency and recommends whether the agency be continued, abolished, or have its role modified is the
    a. Legislative Review Board.
    b. Advisory Commission on Bureau Retention.
    c. Sunset Advisory Commission.
    d. Bureau of Bureaucratic Management.

13. The Texas bureaucracy has continued to proliferate because the legislature and governor have
    a. exercised little, if any, control over the bureaucracy.
    b. allowed state budgets to grow at rates greater than inflation.
    c. yielded to pressures of the federal courts.
    d. followed orders of the Supreme Court of Texas.

14. The Public Utility Commission does *not* have the regulatory power to set rates for
    a. telephone service statewide.
    b. electric service in unincorporated areas.
    c. radio-telephone service statewide.
    d. motor fuel sales.

15. Which of the following is NOT one of the basic policy activities of the Texas bureaucracy?
    a. Serving
    b. Enforcing
    c. Licensing
    d. Promoting

16. According to Professor Charldean Newell, the Texas bureaucracy does its job of administering state government
    a. well above expectations.
    b. poorly.
    c. a little better than average.
    d. well.

17. The mission of the Texas Department of Highways and Public Transportation is to provide
    a. the largest and best system of highways in the nation.
    b. a large budget for building highways in Texas.
    c. safe, effective, and efficient highway transportation for the people of Texas.
    d. a system of highway transportation that allows Texas goods to move from point of manufacture to point of sale quickly and efficiently.

18. After undergoing review by the Sunset Advisory Commission, an agency ceases to exist upon
    a. a three-fourths vote of both houses of the state legislature.
    b. failure of the legislature to renew the agency.
    c. recommendation by the Legislative Budget Board.
    d. a two-thirds vote of the Texas Senate.

Short Answer Question:
19. Describe the purpose of the Sunset review process and evaluate its success.

Answer Key

These are the correct answers with reference to the Learning Objectives, and to the source of the information: the Textbook Focus Points, Jones, *et al. Practicing Texas Politics* (Jones) or Jones, *et. al., Practicing Texas Politics — A Brief Survey* (Survey); the Study Guide Overview (Overview); and the Telelesson Focus Points. Page numbers are also given for the Textbook Focus Points. "KT" indicates questions with Key Terms defined.

Question	Answer	Learning Objective	Textbook Focus Point (page no.)	Telelesson Focus Point
1	B	1	1 (Jones, pp. 319-320; Survey, pp. 206-207)	
2	C	1	1 (Jones, p. 319; Survey, p. 206)	
3	A	2	2 (Jones, pp. 320-322; Survey, pp. 207-208)	
4	D	3	3 (Jones, pp. 322-327; Survey, pp. 208-211)	
5	A	3	3 (Jones, p. 322-324; Survey, p. 208-209)	
6	C	3	4 (Jones, p. 324; Survey, p. 209)	
7	B	3	4 (Jones, p. 324; Survey, p. 210)	
8	D	4	5 (Jones, p. 328; Survey, p. 212)	
9	D	4	5 (Jones, pp. 328-329; Survey, p. 212)	
10	D	4	5 (Jones, p. 328)	
11	B	4	5 (Jones, pp. 334; Survey, p. 215)	
12	C	5	6 (Jones, pp. 340-341; Survey, p. 218) KT	
13	A	5	6 (Jones, pp. 340-341; Survey, p. 218)	
14	D	4	5 (Jones, pp. 329-330; Survey, p. 213)	
15	B	1		1
16	B	1		2
17	C	4		3
18	B	5		4

Short Answer:

| 19 | | 5 | 6 (Jones, pp.340-342; Survey, p. 218) | 4 |

Foreign Policy

Overview

This lesson on making policy differs from the lesson on domestic policy, because here we look at how the U.S. government makes decisions that affect our country's relationships with other countries. Just as domestic policy is an ongoing process, so too is foreign policy. In addition, the concept of trade-offs is as relevant here as it is with domestic policy. Finally, both domestic and foreign policy require negotiation; the difference is that foreign policy must be made with a world neighborhood in mind.

Not too long ago, when we heard the term "foreign policy," we envisioned guns, tanks, and battleships fighting wars. To a large degree, this vision still holds true. So we first examine the war-making powers and duties of both the president and Congress. We study tools the president uses to make these foreign-policy decisions, such as the departments of State and Defense, National Security Council, and Central Intelligence Agency. We also investigate various foreign-policy themes the United States has employed, defining "cold war," "containment," and "detente."

But recently another element has entered the picture: the economy of a nation that relies heavily on foreign trade. We examine the new economic component of foreign policy through a case study dealing with Western Europe and Japan. In the process we question experts about both the trade and the military policies that exist between these areas and the United States, as well as how and why these policies were chosen.

Because the nations of the world are interdependent, one nation's policies can, and usually do, affect the policies of other nations. The effects of the deluge of Japanese cars on the U.S. automotive industry illustrates this well.

Learning Objectives

Goal: The purpose of "Foreign Policy" is to describe why and how the United States develops and implements foreign policy in an interdependent world.

Objectives:

1. Describe U.S. foreign policy–what it is; who makes it; what issues affect it; and its philosophy, major themes, and current challenges.

2. Outline the limitations on a president's war-making powers and what attempts have been made to reduce the nuclear threat.

3. List non-government sources which affect U.S. foreign policy.

4. Compare U.S. trade policy with that of western Europe and of Japan.

5. Contrast U.S. military policy toward western Europe with that toward Japan.

6. Describe how U.S. foreign policy with regard to western Europe and to Japan affects individuals in this country.

Key Terms

Watch for these terms and pay particular attention to what each one means, as you follow the textbook and telelesson.

Foreign policy
Diplomacy
Economic aid
Technical assistance
National security policy
National Security Council
Moral idealism
Political realism
Executive agreement

Intelligence community
Military-industrial complex
Monroe Doctrine
Cold war
Iron curtain
Containment
Detente
Trade deficit (TV)
European Economic Community (TV)

Textbook Reading Assignment

Schmidt, Shelley, and Bardes. *American Government and Politics Today*, 1993-94 edition. Chapter 18, "Foreign and Defense Policy," pp. 593-627.

Textbook Focus Points

Before you read the textbook assignment, review the following points to help focus your thoughts. After you complete the assignment, write out your responses to reinforce what you have learned.

1. What is foreign policy?

2. What has been America's philosophy in foreign policy?

3. Who makes foreign policy?

4. How have the president's war-making powers been limited?

5. What non-governmental sources may influence foreign policy?

6. What have been the major themes of American foreign policy?

7. What are some of the contemporary world problems which affect American foreign policy?

Telelesson Interviewees

The following individuals share their expertise in the telelesson:

Gerald Curtis–Director of East Asian Institute, Columbia University
Marvin Kalb–Professor, Center for Press, Politics, and Public Policy, Harvard University
Rozanne Ridgeway–Assistant Secretary of State, Bureau of European and Canadian Affairs, U.S. Department of State

Telelesson Focus Points

Before viewing the telelesson, read over the following points to help focus your thoughts. After the presentation, write out your responses to help you remember these important points.

1. Who makes foreign policy for the United States?

2. What is the challenge facing today's foreign-policy makers?

3. Describe the U.S. trade policy with western Europe.

4. Describe the U.S. military policy with regard to western Europe.

5. Describe the U.S. trade policy with Japan.

6. Describe the U.S. military policy with regard to Japan.

7. What problems has the United States had with Japan over economic policy?

8. According to Marvin Kalb, how does U.S. foreign policy regarding western Europe and Japan affect us as individuals?

Recommended Reading

The following suggestions are not required unless your instructor assigns them. They are listed to let you know where you can find additional information on areas which interest you.

Alm, Richard. "That Intractable Trade Deficit." *U.S. News & World Report* 101 (September 15, 1986): p. 42.

Clancy, Tom. *Red Storm Rising*. New York: G.P. Putnam's Sons, 1986.

Crabb, Cecil V., and Pat M. Holt. *Invitation to Struggle: Congress, the President and Foreign Policy*. Washington, D.C.: Congressional Quarterly Press, 1980.

Friedman, Milton. "Straight Talk about Deficits." *Reader's Digest* 134 (March 1989): pp. 105-107.

Hattori, Ichiro. "Trade Conflicts: A Japanese View." *Vital Speeches of the Day* 52 (January 15, 1986): pp. 218-221.

Norton, Robert E., and Jack Egan. "Manufacturing a Trade Gap." *U.S. News & World Report* 104 (May 16, 1988): pp.38-39.

Rudolph, Barbara. "A Baffling Trade Imbalance." *Time* 128 (August 11, 1986): pp. 40-42.

Rudolph, Barbara. "Punch in the Eye." *Time* 131 (April 25, 1988): pp. 58-59.

Samuelson, Robert J. "Japan's Case of Malaise." *Newsweek* 109 (May 4, 1987): p.47.

Getting Involved

These activities are not required unless your instructor assigns them. But they offer good suggestions to help you understand and become more involved in the political process.

1. Take a trip to a local variety store or department store. Inspect the labels on a number of items to determine how many are imported and how many are American-made. Closer to home, look around your own home: What kind of car do you drive? What kind of television do you watch? Keep a record, then tally how much you are subtracting from or contributing to the U.S. trade deficit.

2. Note the "Getting Involved" section of your textbook at the end of Chapter 18.

Self Test

After reading the assignment and watching the telelesson, you should be able to answer these questions. When you have completed the test, turn to the Answer Key to score your answers.

1. Foreign policy refers to
   a. the goals a nation wants to achieve, and the techniques and strategies used in trying to achieve them.
   b. formal agreements between nations, which are approved by the World Court.
   c. all actions with other countries that are not related to economics.
   d. only the treaties and executive agreements that are ratified by the Senate.

2. From the earliest years of the republic, Americans have felt that their nation
   a. should have diplomatic ties with every nation.
   b. supplied economic aid to its needy neighbors.
   c. provided technical assistance as we developed it.
   d. had a special destiny.

3. The Constitution created an "invitation to struggle" for control over the foreign-policy process between the
   a. National Security Council and the president.
   b. Department of State and the National Security Council.
   c. president and Congress.
   d. Department of State and Congress.

4. In principle, the State Department is the executive agency that is
   a. directly responsible to Congress.
   b. not involved in short-term foreign policy.
   c. most directly involved with foreign affairs.
   d. responsible for making foreign policy, not the president.

5. In 1973, Congress passed the War Powers Act which
   a. bestowed power on Congress concerning all military actions.
   b. limited the president's use of troops in military action without congressional approval.
   c. extended the president's power to deploy troops as military crises developed.
   d. recognized the increased threat of nuclear war.

6. Which of the following non-governmental sources does NOT influence U.S. foreign policy?
   a. The elite and mass opinion
   b. The military-industrial complex
   c. U.S. multinational business enterprises
   d. The Federal Communications Commission

7. Which of the following has NOT been a major theme of American foreign policy?
   a. Isolationism
   b. Interventionism
   c. Aversion
   d. Internationalism

8. Which of the following is NOT considered a challenge for U.S. foreign policy?
   a. Foreign trade to mainland China
   b. End of the Cold War
   c. Dissolution of the Soviet Union
   d. Political changes in Eastern Europe

9. Constitutional guidelines that make the president the chief foreign-policy maker in the United States do NOT include
   a. being commander in chief.
   b. appointing ambassadors.
   c. appointing justices to the Supreme Court.
   d. negotiating treaties.

10. Which of the following is an ongoing challenge facing today's foreign-policy makers?
   a. Should the Senate ratify SALT II?
   b. How do we balance the U.S. economic and military interests?
   c. Will the U.S. bomb Libya again?
   d. How can we rescue American hostages in Lebanon?

11. The U.S. trade policy with western Europe has resulted in the United States
   a. lowering the price of its exports.
   b. developing a better marketing strategy.
   c. renegotiating its trade agreement.
   d. increasing its trade deficit.

12. In Europe, the United States has been providing one-fourth of the conventional forces and a nuclear arsenal to deter Soviet forces through
   a. NATO.
   b. EEC.
   c. OPEC.
   d. MIRVs.

13. The U.S. trade policy with Japan today allows the Japanese in our markets if they will let us in their markets, emphasizing increased
   a. deficits.
   b. sanctions.
   c. aggression.
   d. reciprocity.

14. Gerald Curtis states that the U.S. military policy with Japan had two objectives: to prevent Japan from being a military power again and to
   a. allow our military forces to be stationed in Japan.
   b. incorporate Japan's fierce warriors into our military.
   c. insure that Japan would be on our side against an adversary.
   d. gain Japan's military bases throughout the Pacific rim.

15. Product "dumping" used by Japan to erect protectionist trade barriers against American-made goods refers to
   a. getting rid of inferior products to reduce losses.
   b. selling below cost to maintain market domination.
   c. putting numerous product samples on the market to determine what the market wants.
   d. sending a new product to a target market.

16. Marvin Kalb states that we are all affected by U.S. foreign policy with western Europe and Japan because
   a. the entire world is hooked into a technological loop.
   b. we all fear a nuclear attack.
   c. so much of our budget is spent on foreign policy.
   d. the U.S. military dominates western Europe and Japan.

Short-Answer Question:
17. Do you believe that the United States should continue to pay large sums of money to maintain the national security of western Europe and Japan while our trade deficit continues to grow? Why or why not?

Answer Key

These are the correct answers with reference to the Learning Objectives, and to the source of the information: the Textbook Focus Points, Schmidt, *et al. American Government and Politics Today* (Schmidt), and the Telelesson Focus Points. Page numbers are also given for the Textbook Focus Points. "KT" indicates questions with Key Terms defined.

Question	Answer	Learning Objective	Textbook Focus Point (page no.)	Telelesson Focus Point
1	A	1	1 (Schmidt, p. 595)............KT	
2	D	1	2 (Schmidt, p. 596)	
3	C	1	3 (Schmidt, p. 598)	
4	C	1	3 (Schmidt, p. 600)	
5	B	2	4 (Schmidt, p. 604)	
6	D	3	5 (Schmidt, p. 605)	
7	C	1	6 (Schmidt, pp. 606-609)	
8	A	1	7 (Schmidt, p. 614)	
9	C	1		1
10	B	1		2
11	D	4		3
12	A	5		4
13	D	4		5
14	C	5		6
15	B	4		7
16	A	6		8

Short Answer:

17		6		8

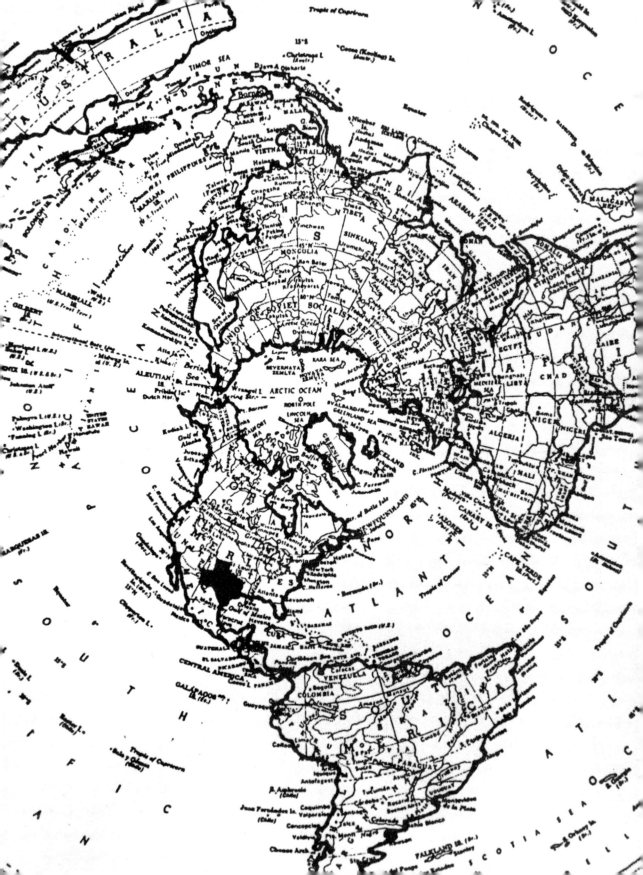

Lesson 14

World Politics: State and Local Perspective

Overview

One of the principal powers of the national government is to conduct relations for the United States with other nations. Only the national government speaks for the nation to the remainder of the world. No state may conduct foreign policy. Nonetheless, states can assist individuals and businesses in their dealings with foreign business by aiding them in opening markets overseas and attracting foreign investment to Texas.

In the 1990s the role of the United States in the world economy is significantly different from the decades after World War II. No longer is the United States the dominant economic power. Currently, Japan and other nations play an equal role. With its diverse economy, Japan is the leading producer of microelectronic technology, steel, and automobiles.

The already powerful role played by western Europe will dramatically increase when the European Economic Community (EEC) or Common Market completes its economic integration. The EEC is scheduled to become a single economic unit with a population larger than the United States, without tariff barriers among member nations and with a unified currency.

Japan is a major economic force in the world today. China, the world's most populous nation, represents a huge, underdeveloped market. South Korea, Taiwan, Thailand, Singapore, and Indonesia are creating modern, industrialized, high-tech markets.

While it is true that no state may formally engage in foreign policy, state and local governments can and do engage in activities to improve the economic climate within a state or local area. In recent years most states have become increasingly active in improving trade by their citizens with other countries.

The Texas Department of Agriculture (TDA) has an International Marketing Program. TDA markets Texas agricultural products around the world. It places foreign buyers in direct contact with sellers in Texas. The TDA has a long-term program with Israel in which Israelis come to Texas to teach desert farming techniques.

In 1989, the Texas legislature authorized the Texas Department of Commerce (TDC) to establish four Texas trade offices overseas. These offices promote Texas products and Texas companies around the world and solicit the relocation of foreign business to Texas. The TDC helps small businesses locate overseas markets and acquire needed export licenses.

The maquiladora, or "twin plant," program was begun by Mexico in 1965 to help alleviate unemployment along the U.S.-Mexican border. It allows a foreign company to establish an assembly or manufacturing operation in Mexico, without having to pay both import and export taxes for components made in the United States and assembled in Mexico for sale outside of Mexico. The assembly process provides work for Mexicans and reduces labor costs for U.S. companies.

Learning Objectives

Goal: The purpose of this lesson is to present an overview of Texas in world economic markets as local, state, and federal branches of government coordinate authority and responsibility.

Objectives:

1. Contrast federal and state authority in establishing business relationships with foreign governments.

2. Describe the changing role of the United States in the world economy since World War II and the emergence of Japan, the European Economic Community, and China as powerful competitors.

3. Explain the role of the Texas Department of Agriculture and the Texas Department of Commerce in expanding Texas markets overseas and in attracting foreign-owned businesses to Texas.

4. Discuss the traditional and currently expanding roles of Texas in world markets.

5. Review the relationship shared by local and state government in the expansion of world markets for Texas products.

Key Terms

Watch for these terms and pay particular attention to what each one means, as you follow the textbook and telelesson.

Texas Department of Agriculture
Texas Department of Commerce
Maquiladora Program

Textbook Reading Assignment

There is no textbook reading assignment for this lesson; however, you are responsible for the information contained in the Study Guide "Overview." There will be overview focus points, self-test questions and questions on your unit examination concerning material found in the Study Guide "Overview."

Overview Focus Points

Before you read the assignment, review the following points to help focus your thoughts. After you complete the assignment, write your responses to reinforce what you have learned.

1. What level of government has the right to conduct relations between the United States and other nations?

2. How has the United States' role in the world economy changed since World War II?

3. Why are Japan, the European Economic Community, and China powerful participants in the world economy?

4. What is the role of the Texas Department of Agriculture and the Texas Department of Commerce in promoting Texas business and products overseas?

Telelesson Interviewees

The following individuals will share their expertise in the telelesson:

Milton Carroll–Commissioner, Port of Houston Authority
Alvin Granoff–Member, Texas House of Representatives, Dallas
Donald Hicks–Department of Political Economy, University of Texas at Dallas
Tom Higgins–Economic Development Director, City of Fort Worth
Patricia Livingston–Texas Department of Commerce

Telelesson Focus Points

Before viewing the telelesson, read the following points to help focus your thoughts. After the presentation, write your responses to help you remember these important points.

1. What restrictions does the national government place on Texas as it does business with foreign business and foreign governments?

2. What has been the traditional role Texas has played in the world marketplace?

3. How has Texas expanded its role in the world marketplace? What Texas-produced goods and services are marketed overseas?

4. What role does the Texas Department of Agriculture and Texas Department of Commerce play in expanding Texas markets and bringing foreign owned businesses to Texas?

5. How do local and state governments cooperate to expand markets?

Recommended Readings

There are no recommended readings for this lesson.

World Politics:
State and Local Perspective

Getting Involved

These activities are not required unless your instructor assigns them. But they offer good suggestions to help you understand and become more involved in the political process.

1. Go to a department store or discount store. Note the number of goods manufactured overseas. Write a report of one or two paragraphs explaining the number and type of foreign-made products you discovered.

2. Carefully monitor news stories for reports of foreign companies located in Texas and Texas companies doing business in other nations.

Self Test

After reading the assignment and watching the telelesson, you should be able to answer these questions. When you have completed the test, turn to the Answer Key to score your answers.

1. The level of government responsible for conducting relations between the United States and other nations is the
   a. national government.
   b. state governments.
   c. regional alliance of states and nations.
   d. local governments.

2. Concerning the role of the United States in the world economy in the 1990s, the United States
   a. is the major economic force in the world.
   b. in partnership with the European Economic Community is the major economic force in the world.
   c. in partnership with Canada and Mexico is the major economic force in the world.
   d. is no longer the major economic force in the world.

3. China is a major economic power in the world due to its
   a. geographic location.
   b. population.
   c. economic diversity.
   d. industrial strength.

4. Japan is a major economic power in the world due to its
   a. geographic location.
   b. population.
   c. large deposits of oil and gold.
   d. economic diversity.

5. In Texas, the state agency responsible for establishing overseas trade offices is the
   a. Texas Department of Resource Development.
   b. Office of Secretary of State.
   c. Texas Department of Commerce.
   d. Office of Economic Development.

6. In Texas, the state agency which develops foreign markets for Texas' agricultural products is the
   a. Texas Department of Resource Development.
   b. Texas Department of Agriculture.
   c. Office of Overseas Development.
   d. Office of Economic Development.

7. Under provisions of the U.S. Constitution, states may not
   a. enter into treaties with foreign governments.
   b. regulate intrastate commerce.
   c. assist businesses in establishing relationships with foreign clients.
   d. allow foreign heads of state to address state legislatures.

8. Texas and Texas businesses have
    a. only recently begun doing business in foreign nations.
    b. not yet firmly established themselves overseas.
    c. little business transactions overseas.
    d. long-standing relationships in foreign markets.

9. For many years, the primary product which Texas marketed in foreign nations was
    a. rice.
    b. oil.
    c. sheep and goats.
    d. peanuts.

10. In the 1980s and 1990s, one product which Texas markets in foreign nations has been
    a. clothing.
    b. computers and computer-related products.
    c. Christmas trees.
    d. gold and silver.

11. The maquiladora program operates plants in Texas and
    a. Canada.
    b. Panama.
    c. Mexico.
    d. Arkansas and Louisiana.

12. In order to attract foreign companies to Texas and to expand markets for Texas goods, the Texas Department of Commerce has established offices in
    a. Japan.
    b. Brazil.
    c. the British Empire.
    d. Burma.

13. The role of local government in attracting foreign companies to Texas and expanding markets for Texas goods is
   a. non-existent.
   b. prohibited under state and federal law.
   c. permitted under federal law, but prohibited under state law.
   d. similar to the role of the state.

Answer Key

These are the correct answers with reference to the Learning Objectives, and to the source of the information: the Textbook Focus Points, Jones, *et al. Practicing Texas Politics* (Jones) or Jones, *et. al., Practicing Texas Politics — A Brief Survey* (Survey); the Study Guide Overview (Overview); and the Telelesson Focus Points. Page numbers are also given for the Textbook Focus Points. "KT" indicates questions with Key Terms defined.

Question	Answer	Learning Objective	Textbook Focus Point (page no.)	Telelesson Focus Point
1	A	1	1 (Overview)	
2	D	2	2 (Overview)	
3	B	2	3 (Overview)	
4	D	2	3 (Overview)	
5	C	3	4 (Overview) KT	
6	B	3	4 (Overview) KT	
7	A	1		1
8	D	4		2
9	B	4		3
10	B	4		3
11	C	3		4
12	A	3		4
13	D	5		5

Lesson 15

The Judiciary

Overview

This lesson and the one on "The Judicial Selection Process" complete our study of the structure of the U.S. government. This lesson focuses on the third branch of government, the judiciary, which—with the executive and legislative branches—forms the three-part system of checks and balances established by the U.S. Constitution. The lessons about the judiciary and the selection process are fundamental to the remaining lessons, about the rights guaranteed by the Constitution that we as Americans enjoy.

Another lesson focuses on how judges are selected. So here we examine the role, structure, and jurisdiction of the federal and state court systems, and find out how cases reach the Supreme Court of the United States. We also analyze how much authority the courts hold in the political process.

Even though the U.S. Constitution established three separate and equal branches of government, in the beginning the judicial branch had to assert itself for equal recognition. It did this with the help of a strong chief justice, John Marshall, and his use of the courts' implied power of judicial review. Some scholars today believe that, through the use of judicial review, the judicial branch has become the most powerful of the three branches.

Except when Supreme Court decisions make headlines, many of us may have little interest in the judiciary. We are apt to view it as just another part of the government, a bunch of stodgy old men in black robes. Not only is that no longer a true description now that women, minorities, and younger people are seated at every level, we also must

---

realize the impact that judicial decisions have on our own lives every day.

Earlier in our study of *Government by Consent* we looked at the historic case of *Brown v. Board of Education of Topeka, Kansas*. Here we examine how this case affected the lives of many people, as well as how it brought up another educational issue: busing. We hear from real people who took the busing issue to the Supreme Court and listen to them tell about their personal experiences and reactions to the Court's decision.

In many ways the judiciary certainly is the least visible and least understood branch of government. But the influence of the judicial branch is profound, and the impact of its decisions often last for many generations.

Learning Objectives

Goal: The purpose of "The Judiciary" is to describe the state and federal court systems, including methods of getting cases to the Supreme Court, how the judiciary influences the political process, and the ways its decisions affect each of us every day.

Objectives:

1. Review the British system upon which most U.S. law is based, including the function of *stare decisis* in the judicial system.

2. Describe the decision-making process of Supreme Court judges, citing precedent and other sources which form the bases for their decisions.

3. Detail the basic structure of the federal and state judicial systems, including the checks placed on the judicial branch.

---

4. Describe the types of cases that reach the U.S. Supreme Court and the kinds of opinions that form the final decisions.

5. Explain the strategies used by individuals and interest groups to try to influence the judicial system, especially in the case brought by the citizens of Mecklenburg County, North Carolina, in 1965.

6. Show how decisions of the U.S. Supreme Court affect individuals, citing examples from both popular and unpopular court decisions.

7. List the weaknesses of the Supreme Court expressed by Patrick Higgenbotham.

8. Explain judicial review and how it was established.

9. Outline what goes into any judge's decision-making process.

Key Terms

Watch for these terms and pay particular attention to what each one means, as you follow the textbook and telelesson.

Common law	**Opinion**
Precedent	**Majority opinion**
Stare decisis	**Concurring opinion**
Judicial review	**Dissenting opinion**
Original jurisdiction	*Amicus curiae* **briefs**
Trial courts	**Class-action suit**
Jurisdiction	**Political question**
Appellate courts	**Judicial implementation**
Writ of certiorari	

Textbook Reading Assignment

Schmidt, Shelley, and Bardes. *American Government and Politics Today*, 1993-94 edition. Chapter 15, "The Judiciary," pp. 493-508, 520-525.

Textbook Focus Points

Before you read the textbook assignment, review the following points to help focus your thoughts. After you complete the assignment, write out your responses to reinforce what you have learned.

1. On what system is most American law based, and what function does *stare decisis* serve in the American judicial system?

2. What sources other than precedent do the courts consider when making their decisions?

3. What is the basic structure of America's judicial system today?

4. Which cases reach the U.S. Supreme Court, and what types of opinions form the final decisions?

5. How do interest groups participate in the judicial system?

6. What checks are placed on the judicial branch in order to keep our system of government balanced?

Telelesson Interviewees

The following individuals share their expertise in the telelesson:

Reginald Hawkins–Original Plaintiff in *Swann v. Mecklenburg*
Patrick Higgenbotham–Judge, 5th U.S. Circuit Court of Appeals
Arthur R. Miller–Professor, Harvard University Law School
Pauline Paddock–Columnist, *Charlotte Observer*, Charlotte, North
  Carolina
Barefoot Sanders– U.S. District Judge, Northern District of Texas
John R. Schmidhauser–Professor of Political Science, University of
  Southern California

Telelesson Focus Points

Before viewing the telelesson, read over the following points to help
focus your thoughts. After the presentation, write out your responses
to help you remember these important points.

1. Describe the basic structure of the federal courts and the state
   courts.
2. How does the U.S. Supreme Court impact American society, and
   what are some examples that illustrate this?

3. According to Patrick Higgenbotham, what are some weaknesses
   of the Supreme Court?

4. What is judicial review, and how was it established?

5. How did the citizens of Mecklenburg County in Charlotte, North
   Carolina, in 1965 use the courts to accomplish their goals?

6. What influences a judge's decision-making process?

7. Why do people comply with unpopular court decisions?

8. How does Arthur Miller believe the Supreme Court affects the lives of individuals, and why does he call the Supreme Court the "glue" that holds the American enterprise together?

Recommended Reading

The following suggestions are not required unless your instructor assigns them. They are listed to let you know where you can find additional information on areas which interest you.

Abraham, Henry. *The Judicial Process: An Introductory Analysis of the Courts of the United States, England, and France,* 5th edition. New York: Oxford University Press, 1986.

Friedman, Lawrence M. "Judges and Courts: 1850-1900," in *A History of American Law,* 2nd edition. New York: Simon & Schuster, 1985, pp. 371-390.

Harrell, Mary Ann; Burnett Anderson; and the National Geographic Staff. *Equal Justice Under Law: The Supreme Court in American Life.* Washington, D.C.: The Supreme Court Historical Society, 1988.

O'Brien, David M. *Storm Center: Supreme Court in American Politics.* New York: W.W. Norton and Company, 1986.

Tribe, Lawrence. *God Save This Honorable Court.* New York: Random House, 1985.

Getting Involved

These activities are not required unless your instructor assigns them. But they offer good suggestions to help you understand and become more involved in the political process.

1. Note the "Getting Involved" section of your textbook at the end of Chapter 15.

2. Visit a local district court, and write a brief essay evaluating the procedures and organization that you observed.

Self Test

After reading the assignment and watching the telelesson, you should be able to answer these questions. When you have completed the test, turn to the Answer Key to score your answers.

1. Most of American law is based on
   a. Roman law.
   b. English common law.
   c. doctrines of Friedrich Engels.
   d. French civil law.

2. Which of the following is NOT a function of *stare decisis*?
   a. It helps the courts to be more efficient.
   b. It makes a more uniform judicial system.
   c. It makes the law more stable and predictable.
   d. It provides a legal system without bias toward the wealthy.

3. In making decisions, which of the following sources is least likely to be considered by the courts?
   a. Precedent
   b. Constitutions
   c. Public opinion
   d. Statutes

4. The United States has a dual court system of
   a. civil courts and criminal courts.
   b. state courts and federal courts.
   c. misdemeanor courts and felony courts.
   d. state courts and local courts.

5. In the majority of cases it hears, the Supreme Court today rarely acts as a court of original jurisdiction, but rather as
   a. an appellate court.
   b. a trial court.
   c. a criminal court.
   d. a civil court.

6. Interest groups play an important role in our judicial system, because they
   a. can veto judicial nominations.
   b. help to fund the judicial review board.
   c. perform a constitutional duty.
   d. litigate cases.

7. Which of these does NOT serve as a check on the judicial system?
   a. The legislative branch
   b. The executive branch
   c. The general public
   d. The military

8. The major impact of the Supreme Court on American society is through
   a. ruling on civil matters.
   b. decisions on criminal matters.
   c. interpretation of the U.S. Constitution.
   d. judicial review of state constitutions.

9. Patrick Higgenbotham describes the Supreme Court as the least dangerous branch of the U.S. government because
   a. it lacks the power of enforcement.
   b. its members go through the confirmation process.
   c. it depends on Congress to determine its jurisdiction.
   d. the president can alter its philosophical foundation.

10. The Supreme Court asserted its right to reject actions of the executive and legislative branches of government and the lower courts in a concept called
    a. *stare decisis*.
    b. common law.
    c. judicial review.
    d. writ of certiorari.

11. After the parents of a black child filed a lawsuit in 1965 against Mecklenburg County School District to allow their son to attend a predominantly white school near his home, the federal district court judge ordered the school district to
    a. allow the child to attend the location of his choice.
    b. bus 10,000 students for the sole purpose of racial desegregation.
    c. provide transportation to the child's original assignment.
    d. determine how many other black children wanted to attend the white school.

12. According to Barefoot Sanders, judges make their decisions consciously, by following legal precedents, and subconsciously, as a result of the judge's
    a. religious beliefs.
    b. judicial training and political philosophy.
    c. background, experiences, and personal values.
    d. legal experiences and educational background.

13. The issue of school desegregation shows that even after Supreme Court rulings, compliance
    a. cannot be forced.
    b. has to be voluntary.
    c. is carried out by the district courts.
    d. may be slow and painful.

14. Arthur Miller calls the Supreme Court the "glue" that holds the American enterprise together, because it
    a. brokers the fight that develops between Congress and the presidency.
    b. is composed of members who are appointed and not partners in the partisan battle.
    c. has to depend on Congress and the president to implement its decisions.
    d. involves lifetime appointments away from the electoral frenzy.

Short-Answer Question:

15. What role do you believe the federal judiciary should play in the lives of individuals? Why?

Answer Key

These are the correct answers with reference to the Learning Objectives, and to the source of the information: the Textbook Focus Points, Schmidt, *et al. American Government and Politics Today* (Schmidt), and the Telelesson Focus Points. Page numbers are also given for the Textbook Focus Points. "KT" indicates questions with Key Terms defined.

Question	Answer	Learning Objective	Textbook Focus Point (page no.)	Telelesson Focus Point
1.	B	1	1 (Schmidt, p. 495)............KT	
2.	D	1	1 (Schmidt, pp. 495-496)..KT	
3.	C	2	2 (Schmidt, pp. 496-497)	
4.	B	3	3 (Schmidt, p. 500)	1
5.	A	4	4 (Schmidt, p. 503)............KT	
6.	D	5	5 (Schmidt, p. 505)	
7.	D	3	6 (Schmidt, p. 520)	
8.	C	6		2
9.	A	7		3
10.	C	8	KT	4
11.	B	5		5
12.	C	9		6
13.	D	6		7
14.	A	6		8

Short Answer:

15.		6	5 (Schmidt, p. 505-508)	2,7,8

CRIMINAL DISTRICT COURT 5
282nd & 363rd DISTRICT COURT
AUXILIARY COURT 1

Lesson 16

Texas Civil and Criminal Law

Overview

The ultimate penalty that society can extract from an individual is the forfeiture of that person's life. Like many other states, Texas imposes a death penalty for certain crimes. Since Texas' death penalty statute was upheld by the United States Supreme Court, Texas has executed more men than any other state. Texas also has more people awaiting execution than any other state.

This program discusses the death penalty, offers arguments in support of it, and considers reasons against it. Does a government have the right to take a life? This is a question which each of us, as a member of society, must answer for ourself.

A capital offense is any crime for which the death penalty is possible. Those individuals convicted of a capital offense face life in prison or death by lethal injection. Texas has six other degrees of crimes, ranging from Class C misdemeanors to first degree felonies. Punishments range from a small fine to life imprisonment and a $10,000 fine.

Civil law is the body of rules and regulations which direct the relationship between individuals. Among other things, civil law regulates marriage, divorce, banking, property, and child custody.

There are six main courts in the Texas judicial system. Three are called courts of original jurisdiction: justice of the peace courts, county courts including county courts at law, and district courts. Three are known as courts of appellate jurisdiction: courts of appeals, the Texas Court of Criminal Appeals, and the Supreme Court of Texas. Courts of original jurisdiction have both civil and criminal jurisdiction, as do the courts of appeals. The Texas Court of Criminal Appeals is Texas' highest criminal court. The Supreme Court of Texas has no criminal jurisdiction, but it is the state's highest civil court.

In Texas, state court judges are elected in partisan elections. This lesson describes the advantages and disadvantages of electing, rather than appointing, our state's judges. A question of propriety is raised when judges must campaign and seek campaign funds from attorneys—the very people who appear before judges. The video program also analyzes whether appointment or election of judges produces better justice.

Learning Objectives

Goal: The goal of this lesson is to describe the court system in Texas as it relates to both civil and criminal law.

Objectives:

1. Identify the characteristics which differentiate civil law and criminal law in Texas.

2. Outline the differences in crimes, possible fines, periods of confinement, and courts with original and appellate jurisdiction that are associated with both felonies and misdemeanors in Texas.

3. Contrast the advantages and disadvantages of plea bargaining and out-of-court settlements versus trials.

4. Discuss arguments for and against allowing the death penalty in Texas, including crimes, alternate punishments, and jury deliberations.

5. Describe the roles of judges and justices in the court system of Texas, particularly in regard to qualifications, terms of office, jurisdiction, professional conduct, and campaign strategies.

6. Evaluate the legal system of Texas as it operates in enforcing the law and bringing criminals to justice.

Key Terms

Watch for these terms and pay particular attention to what each one means, as you follow the textbook and telelesson.

Civil law	**Capital felony**
Criminal law	**Trial** *de novo*
Common law	**Justice of the peace**
Penal code	**District Court**
Original jurisdiction	**Constitutional county court**
Appellate jurisdiction	**Courts of appeals**
Felony	**Court of Criminal Appeals**
Misdemeanor	**Supreme Court of Texas**

Textbook Reading Assignment

Jones, Ericson, Brown, and Trotter. *Practicing Texas Politics*, 8th edition. Chapter 8, "Law, Courts, and Justice," pp. 361-420, especially pp. 361-390 and 397-413.

Jones, Ericson, Brown, Trotter, and Lynch. *Practicing Texas Politics – A Brief Survey*, 4th edition. Chapter 8, "Law, Courts, and Justice," pp. 222-261, especially pp. 222-244 and 253-261.

Note to students: You are responsible for only *one* of these reading assignments. It is your responsibility to know which book is used in your class.

Textbook Focus Points

Before you read the textbook assignment, review the following points to help focus your thoughts. After you complete the assignment, write your responses to reinforce what you have learned.

1. What is the difference between civil law and criminal law in Texas?

2. What are the differences between felonies and misdemeanors? What are the differences in crimes, possible fines, periods of confinement, and courts with original jurisdiction among Class A, Class B, and Class C misdemeanors? What are the differences among first degree, second degree, and third degree felonies in reference to specific crimes, possible fines, period of confinement, and court(s) with original jurisdiction?

3. What are the crimes for which the death penalty is possible in Texas? Identify possible punishments for capital felonies. Specify the questions a jury must answer before sentencing a defendant to death.

4. What are the qualifications and terms of office for judges or justices in Texas? What is the jurisdiction of each of the following courts: justice of the peace court (including small claims court), constitutional county courts, county courts at law, district courts, criminal district courts, courts of appeals, the Court of Criminal Appeals, and the Supreme Court of Texas?

5. Discuss the cases of innocent people convicted and sentenced to prison in Texas.

6. Describe the election of judges in Texas and the problems associated with that system.

Telelesson Interviewees

The following individuals will share their expertise in the telelesson:

Randall Dale Adams–Wrongly convicted of a capital offense; subject of the film, *Thin Blue Line*

Karyne Conley–Member, Texas House of Representatives, San Antonio

Robert Diaz–Assistant City Attorney, Arlington, Texas

John Hill–Former Chief Justice, Supreme Court of Texas

Jim Mattox–Former Attorney General of Texas

Oscar Mauzy–Former Associate Justice, Supreme Court of Texas

Erroll Morris–Filmmaker

Tom Phillips–Chief Justice, Supreme Court of Texas

Randy Shafer–Attorney for Randall Dale Adams

John Vance–District Attorney, Dallas County

Mark White–Former Governor of Texas

Telelesson Focus Points

Before viewing the telelesson, read the following points to help focus your thoughts. After the presentation, write your responses to help you to remember these important points.

1. What are the arguments for and against the death penalty?

2. What are the advantages and disadvantages of plea bargains and out-of-court settlements?

3. How are state court judges selected in Texas? What are arguments in favor of partisan judicial elections?

4. According to Oscar Mauzy, what difference is there in the quality of justice when judges are elected or appointed?

Recommended Reading

The following suggestions are not required unless your instructor assigns them. They are listed to let you know where you can find additional information on areas which interest you.

Alderman, Richard M. *Know Your Rights: Answers to Texans' Everyday Legal Questions.* Houston: Gulf Publishing Company, 1986.

Barrett, William P. "The Best Justice Money Can Buy." *Forbes* (June 1, 1987): pp. 122, 126.
Case, Ken. "Blind Justice." *Texas Monthly* (May 1987): pp. 136-138, 195-198.

Dugger, Ronnie. "In the Dead of the Night." *Texas Observer* (April 22, 1988): pp. 1, 7-9.

Hart, Patricia Kilday. "Disorder in the Court." *Texas Monthly* (March 1988): pp. 118-120.

Johnson, Amy. "Court Reform? The Case Against the Appointment of Judges." *Texas Observer* (February 6, 1987): pp. 8-10.

Getting Involved

This activity is not required unless your instructor assigns it. But it offers good suggestions to help you understand and become more involved in the political process.

> Attend a day or more of a civil or criminal trial held in a state district court. Write a paper of at least one page in which you describe what happened and your reactions to the trial.

Self Test

After reading the assignment and watching the telelesson, you should be able to answer these questions. When you have completed the test, turn to the Answer Key to score your answers.

1. The part of the law dealing with private actions and relationships among individuals is known as
    a. civil law.
    b. criminal law.
    c. common law.
    d. special law.

2. Texas laws defining crimes and prescribing punishments are found in the state's
    a. Penal Code.
    b. Code of the West.
    c. Code of Criminal Procedure.
    d. Civil Code.

3. A court hearing a dispute over a contract is exercising
    a. civil jurisdiction.
    b. criminal jurisdiction.
    c. common jurisdiction.
    d. special jurisdiction.

4. A less serious crime for which the maximum penalty in Texas is a fine and no more than one year in the county jail is known as a
    a. felony.
    b. county offense.
    c. misdemeanor.
    d. litigant.

5. In Texas, which of the following courts exercises original jurisdiction over Class A and Class B misdemeanors?
   a. Justice of the Peace Court
   b. Constitutional County Court
   c. District Court
   d. Municipal Court

6. In Texas, which of the following is the most serious classification of crime?
   a. Class C misdemeanor
   b. Class A misdemeanor
   c. Third degree felony
   d. First degree felony

7. After a Texas jury has found a defendant guilty of a capital offense, it must then decide whether the
   a. the defendant is a minor.
   b. offender had been abused as a child.
   c. victim and the offender were of the same race and ethnic group.
   d. defendant is likely to commit criminal acts of violence that would constitute a continuing threat to society.

8. In less populated counties in Texas, justices of the peace may also determine the cause of death in their function as
   a. medical examiner.
   b. coroner.
   c. foremen of grand juries.
   d. county funeral director.

9. You rented an apartment in McAllen. When you signed your lease, you gave the manager a $200 deposit, refundable at the conclusion of the lease, assuming that you leave the apartment in good condition. Your lease is now up, and you have moved out and left the apartment in good condition. Your ex-landlord, however, is refusing to return your deposit. In what court would you file suit against the landlord?
   a. County court.
   b. Justice of the peace court.
   c. District court.
   d. Municipal court.

10. The Supreme Court of Texas hears an appeal from a court of appeals when
   a. capital punishment is involved.
   b. legislative acts have been held unconstitutional.
   c. either party is dissatisfied with the decision of the lower court.
   d. the case involves an agency within the executive branch.

11. The highest criminal court in Texas is the
   a. State District Court.
   b. Texas Court of Appeals.
   c. Texas Court of Criminal Appeals.
   d. Texas Supreme Court.

12. In a criminal trial in Texas
   a. the punishment is automatically set when the jury returns a guilty verdict.
   b. a separate hearing must be held to assess the penalty.
   c. the prosecuting attorney may waive trial by jury.
   d. a simple majority vote by the jury is sufficient to convict the accused person.

13. Under Texas law, a person observed by a police officer to be drinking while driving on a public highway is committing a (Jones, 8th ed.)
    a. Class A misdemeanor.
    b. Class B misdemeanor.
    c. Class C misdemeanor.
    d. felony.

14. Which of the following is NOT true of plea bargains and out-of-court settlements?
    a. They save the time of the courts.
    b. They provide easier and speedier access to courts for other individuals.
    c. They represent less costly methods for resolving conflicts.
    d. They result in longer sentences and higher awards.

15. In Texas, state judges are
    a. elected by the citizens of Texas.
    b. appointed by the governor of Texas.
    c. appointed by the chief justice of the Supreme Court of Texas.
    d. appointed by the attorney-general of Texas.

16. When comparing the quality of justice in courts where the judge was appointed, with the quality where the judge was elected, it has been determined that justice is
    a. more nearly met in courts where the judge is appointed.
    b. more nearly met in courts where the judge is elected.
    c. the same quality regardless of the method of selection of judges.
    d. more nearly met when judges are appointed at the appellate level and elected in courts of original jurisdiction.

Short -Answer Question:
17. Briefly discuss two arguments for the death penalty and two arguments against the death penalty.

Answer Key

These are the correct answers with reference to the Learning Objectives, and to the source of the information: the Textbook Focus Points, Jones, *et al. Practicing Texas Politics* (Jones) or Jones, *et. al., Practicing Texas Politics — A Brief Survey* (Survey); the Study Guide Overview (Overview); and the Telelesson Focus Points. Page numbers are also given for the Textbook Focus Points. "KT" indicates questions with Key Terms defined.

Question	Answer	Learning Objective	Textbook Focus Point (page no.)	Telelesson Focus Point
1	A	1	1 (Jones, p. 385; Survey, p.241)...............KT	
2	A	1	1 (Jones, p. 365; Survey, p. 226)...............KT	
3	A	1	1 (Jones, p. 365; Survey, p. 226)	
4	C	2	2 (Jones, pp. 365-366; Survey, pp. 226-227).....KT	
5	B	2	2 (Jones, p. 374; Survey, p. 233)	
6	D	2	2 (Jones, p. 366; Survey, p. 227)	
7	D	4	3 (Jones, p. 368; Survey, p. 228)	
8	B	5	4 (Jones, p. 373; Survey, p. 232)	
9	B	5	4 (Jones, pp. 371-373; Survey, pp. 231-232)	
10	B	5	4 (Jones, p. 380; Survey, p. 237)	
11	C	5	4 (Jones, p. 378; Survey, pp. 236-237)	
12	B	2	4 (Jones, pp. 388-389; Survey, p. 244)	
13	C	2	2 (Jones, pp. 366-367)	
14	D	3		2
15	A	5		3
16	C	5		4

Short Answer:

17		4		1

York Times

LATE CITY EDIT

Weather: Mostly sunny toda
tonight. Mostly sunny tor
Temperature range: today
yesterday 74-94. Details on p

WEDNESDAY, JULY 8, 1981

30 cents beyond 80-mile zone from New York City.
Higher in air delivery cities.

25 CE

CY
AD
RMS

eller

eagan
ource
ed to
apons
be a
plier
d pur-

eight-
n pro-
d sub-
White
efore
. The
one of

ched
inis-
ct a
the
was
aign
ition
s in

off-
there

d of
eaf-

REAGAN NOMINATING WOMAN
AN ARIZONA APPEALS JUDGE
TO SERVE ON SUPREME COUR

REACTION IS MI

Senate Seems Favo
but Opposition Aris
on Abortion Stand

By STEVEN R. WEISSMAN
Special to The New York Times

WASHINGTON, July 7 — Pre
Reagan announced today that he
nominate Sandra Day O'Connor
year-old judge on the Arizona C
Appeals, to the United States Su
Court. If confirmed, she would b
the first woman to serve on the Co

"She is truly a 'person f
seasons,'" Mr. Reagan said this
ing, "possessing those unique qu
of temperament, fairness, intell

Remarks on Court post, page A

capacity and devotion to the public
which have characterized the 101
ren' who have preceded her."

White House and Justice Depa
officials expressed confidence
Judge O'Connor's views were co
ible with those espoused over the
by Mr. Reagan, who has been
critical of some past Supreme

Lesson 17

The Judicial Selection Process

Overview

Judges have been described as guardians of all the legal rights that the U.S. Constitution guarantees to every citizen. In some judicial decisions, judges have the power to decide between life and death for the accused; in many cases, their rulings set precedent or decide an issue in a way other judges can follow for generations. This lesson describes the characteristics of the people who become judges and explains how they reach that position.

We begin by seeing how judgeships are filled: via election, appointment, or a combination of the two. Judicial experts discuss the advantages and disadvantages of each method of selection.

Although the process for selecting state judges varies from state to state, the election of judges is still popular in many states. But all federal judges are appointed, so we examine that process next, along with the pros and cons of the appointive system. Finally, as we realize that federal judges are appointed for life and that their decisions impact our own lives for generations, we see how imperative it is that only the best qualified people be appointed.

Judicial scholars characterize judges as being activist or restraintist, or as liberal and conservative, because judges bring to the bench their own philosophies, education, and personal experiences. As we examine the appointment of Robert Bork to the Supreme Court, followed by the enormous controversy surrounding the confirmation process, we especially note the reasoning behind Judge Bork's interpretations of the Constitution while he served on the federal circuit court of appeals.

How judges are selected is vitally important, because their decisions have such a far-reaching influence on our lives. Even so, judges are human like the rest of us. The most difficult part of a judge's job is to judge a case on its own merits and not be guided unduly by his or her personal views and philosophies—or even by public outcry. For a judge's overriding goal must be to provide justice for everyone.

Learning Objectives

Goal: The purpose of "The Judicial Selection Process" is to describe the appointive and elective systems of selecting judges, while suggesting ways that individuals can be involved in either procedure.

Objectives:

1. Describe the nomination process for federal judges, as well as the characteristics most likely to be associated with federal and Supreme Court justices.

2. Outline the qualifications required to become a federal judge and how the judicial selection process works, including the importance of the ideology of the candidates and of those who appoint them.

3. Define judicial activism and judicial restraint, and illustrate how these terms apply to the federal judiciary.

4. Explain what judges do while the various courts are in session.

5. Evaluate the two different methods used to select state judges, including some of the problems inherent in each method.

6. List the basic steps for filling a vacancy on the federal bench, and explain the impact of the lifetime term on this process.

7. Describe the opportunities that individuals have to affect the judicial selection process.

Key Terms

Watch for these terms and pay particular attention to what each one means, as you follow the textbook and telelesson.

Senatorial courtesy   **Judicial selection (TV)**
Judicial activism   **Litigious society (TV)**
Judicial restraint

Textbook Reading Assignment

Schmidt, Shelley, and Bardes. *American Government and Politics Today*, 1993-94 edition. Chapter 15, "The Judiciary," pp. 508-520.

Textbook Focus Points

Before you read the textbook assignment, review the following points to help focus your thoughts. After you complete the assignment, write out your responses to reinforce what you have learned.

1. How does the nomination process for federal judges work?

2. What role does ideology play in the judicial selection process?

3. What characteristics are most likely to describe a federal judge or Supreme Court justice?

4. What are the qualifications of federal judges?

5. What are "judicial activism" and "judicial restraint" as these terms apply to the federal judicial system?

Telelesson Interviewees

The following individuals share their expertise in the telelesson:

Anthony Champagne–Professor of Political Economy, University of Texas, Dallas
Arthur R. Miller–Professor, Harvard University Law School
Tom Phillips–Chief Justice, Supreme Court of Texas

Telelesson Focus Points

Before viewing the telelesson, read over the following points to help focus your thoughts. After the presentation, write out your responses to help you remember these important points.

1. What is meant by the term "judicial selection," and why is it important?

2. What do judges do while the various courts are in session?

3. How are state judges selected, and what are some of the problems inherent in the elective method?

4. How long is a federal judge's term of office, and what are the arguments in favor of this type of term?

5. What are the basic steps for filling a vacancy on the federal bench?

6. When and how can individuals affect the process of judicial selection?

Recommended Reading

The following suggestions are not required unless your instructor assigns them. They are listed to let you know where you can find additional information on areas which interest you.

Kramer, Michael. "The Brief on Judge Bork." *U.S. News & World Report* 103 (September 14, 1987): pp. 18-24.

Lamar, Jacob V. "Advise and Dissent." *Time* 130 (September 21, 1987): pp. 12-18+.
Press, Aric. "Trying to Leave a Conservative Legacy." *Newsweek* 110 (July 13, 1987): pp. 22-23.

Woodward, Bob, and Scott Armstrong. *The Brethren: Inside the Supreme Court*. New York: Simon and Schuster, 1979.

Getting Involved

These activities are not required unless your instructor assigns them. But they offer good suggestions to help you understand and become more involved in the political process.

1. Select a former or current justice of the U.S. Supreme Court, develop a brief biographical sketch of that justice, and analyze the justice's impact on the Court.

2. Much has been written both criticizing and praising Chief Justice Earl Warren. At one point during his term, there was a movement to impeach him! Research the decisions made by that court, then write a brief essay giving your opinions about Earl Warren and the decisions of that court. Do you think he and his court were too liberal? Should he have been impeached, or was he merely bringing the Supreme Court into the mid-twentieth century?

Self Test

After reading the assignment and watching the telelesson, you should be able to answer these questions. When you have completed the test, turn to the Answer Key to score your answers.

1. Although the president nominates federal judges, the nomination of district court judges typically originates with
   a. the state's governor if from the president's political party.
   b. a senator or senators of the president's party.
   c. members of the House of Representatives from the state where the vacancy occurs.
   d. state bar association in the state where the vacancy occurs.

2. An important factor in the president's choices for the federal judiciary and in the Senate confirmation hearings that follow is the candidate's
   a. occupation.
   b. religion.
   c. age.
   d. ideology.

3. The only relatively predictable characteristic of Supreme Court appointments is that the nominees will be from the same
   a. region of the country as the president.
   b. religious denomination as the president.
   c. age group as the president.
   d. political party as the president.

4. Most federal judges have had experience
   a. as a state judge.
   b. at some level of government.
   c. in an elective office.
   d. teaching in a law school.

5. Judicial scholars like to characterize different Supreme Courts and various Supreme Court justices by how they
   a. view the Constitution and become involved in matters affecting the other branches of government.
   b. write their opinions and how often they are in the majority.
   c. react to public opinion and incorporate it in their decisions.
   d. interact with the other justices and argue their different views.

6. The public's low awareness and lack of involvement in the judicial selection process is a concern because the judiciary
   a. receives large amounts of federal appropriations.
   b. is in session all year.
   c. makes decisions that affect our lives daily.
   d. is confirmed by the House of Representatives.

7. Which one of the following is NOT a judge's responsibility in a court of original jurisdiction?
   a. To determine whether a trial has been conducted properly
   b. To rule on the kinds of evidence that can be introduced
   c. To decide guilt or innocence
   d. To set punishment in a criminal case

8. Which of the following is NOT a method of selecting state judges?
   a. Appointed by the governor with the consent of the legislature
   b. Elected in general elections
   c. Appointed by the House and confirmed by the Senate
   d. Selected by a combination of appointment and election

9. Federal judges are appointed by the president and confirmed by the Senate to serve a
   a. single six-year term.
   b. four-year term, subject to reappointment.
   c. five-year term, eligible to serve a total of twenty years.
   d. lifetime term.

10. When there is a vacancy on a federal district court, the president may select a candidate using the system of
   a. presidential prerogative.
   b. senatorial courtesy.
   c. senatorial privilege.
   d. executive order.

11. Individuals and groups have an opportunity to give their views on a Supreme Court nominee
   a. before the president sends a nomination to the Senate Judiciary Committee.
   b. during the public hearings held by the Senate Judiciary Committee.
   c. before the House of Representatives votes to confirm or reject a nominee.
   d. before the nominee is sworn in before a joint session of Congress.

Short-Answer Question:
12. If you had served on the Senate Judiciary Committee during Robert Bork's hearings, would you have voted to confirm or reject his nomination? Why?

Answer Key

These are the correct answers with reference to the Learning Objectives, and to the source of the information: the Textbook Focus Points, Schmidt, *et al. American Government and Politics Today* (Schmidt), and the Telelesson Focus Points. Page numbers are also given for the Textbook Focus Points. "KT" indicates questions with Key Terms defined.

Question	Answer	Learning Objective	Textbook Focus Point (page no.)	Telelesson Focus Point
1.	B	1	1 (Schmidt, p.509)	
2.	D	2	2 (Schmidt, p.511)	
3.	D	1	3 (Schmidt, p.511)	
4.	B	2	4 (Schmidt, pp.514-515)	
5.	A	3	5 (Schmidt, p.517)	
6.	C	2		1
7.	A	4		2
8.	C	5		3
9.	D	6		4
10.	B	6	1 (Schmidt, p.509)	KT	5
11.	B	7		6

Short Answer:

12.		2		1,5

Lesson 18

Texas Criminal Justice System

Overview

The criminal justice system is of vital importance to everyone. Each year, one-third of all Texans become victims of crime. Homicide is the second leading cause of death among young male Texans between the ages of eighteen and thirty-four. And, the crime rate in Texas has doubled in less than fifteen years.

Consequently, the Texas criminal justice system is overwhelmed by the increasing numbers of people entering the system. This has produced a backlog of cases to be tried in metropolitan areas. It also has resulted in overcrowded prisons, overworked parole and probation officers, too few half-way houses for the number of people who could benefit from them for part of their prison time, and a growing reluctance on the part of state officials to appropriate the money necessary for the criminal justice system to perform as it should.

A person's involvement with the Texas criminal justice system begins when that individual commits a crime and subsequently is arrested. If convicted, the state's involvement doesn't end until the person is completely released. Between arrest and final release, the major elements of the criminal justice system include: arraignment, indictment, trial, sentencing, probation or incarceration, and parole.

In Texas' metropolitan areas, it is common for accused individuals to wait up to a year for a jury trial. Also, in the more populous areas, those persons placed on probation receive little supervision, because the probation system is so overworked and overcrowded. In the telelesson Ron Chapman, a state district judge from Dallas County, and Harris County District Attorney Johnny Holmes describe the problems caused by crowded criminal dockets. They offer alternatives to the present system from the perspective of people who see the criminal justice system operate firsthand.

Under an agreement with the federal courts, Texas prisons may not exceed ninety-five percent of capacity. But so many people are being sentenced by Texas juries to the Texas Department of Criminal Justice (TDCJ) that, regardless of the length of the sentence, the time spent in the state prison system must be shortened.

Criminals sentenced to twenty years in prison may serve only three or four years. In 1990, individuals who had been sentenced to life in prison were being incarcerated an average of less than ten years. People sentenced to brief terms, who remained in the county jail while awaiting trial, may never see the state prison system. Others go to a state prison only long enough to be processed out of the system.

In the video, Hidalgo County Sheriff Edgar Ruiz illustrates the impact of prison overcrowding and its effect on county officials. Marshall Herklotz, an administrator with the TDCJ, examines the effect of prison overcrowding. State Representative Alan Hightower of Huntsville reviews some proposed legislative solutions to TDCJ problems.

One objective of the criminal justice system and the TDCJ is to rehabilitate people convicted of crimes, in order to keep them from returning to prison. A huge proportion of crimes committed in Texas are related to the use of drugs or alcohol, and a large proportion of TDCJ inmates are high school dropouts, functionally illiterate, and have no marketable skills.

TDCJ rehabilitation programs include drug and alcohol counseling, but funding is so limited that new arrivals must go on a waiting list for this counseling. Other rehabilitation offered includes learning basic skills such as reading and writing, obtaining a high school diploma from the Windham Independent School District (operated entirely by the TDCJ to educate inmates), attending junior college, or receiving practical and marketable vocational training. But when stays in the TDCJ are shortened, rehabilitation is short-circuited.

Prisoners must be released early from the TDCJ to make room for new inmates. Yet many of those freed on parole go into another overcrowded system. Parole officers in metropolitan areas supervise two and one-half to three times the number of offenders that experts believe can be supervised effectively. The result is that parolees receive little supervision and scant help.

One way to improve the criminal justice system in Texas is to shorten the time between arrest and trial. Many experts believe that swift, sure punishment is more effective than a harsh sentence imposed long after a crime has been committed. To accomplish this requires more judges, more district attorneys, more court staff, and more courtrooms.

But some creative problem solving could reduce some of these costs. For example, trials could be conducted from late afternoon into the evening and almost double the number of trials conducted in the same physical space.

The number of parole and probation officers must be increased, too, in order to bring the number of people supervised down to a reasonable number. This would allow probationers and parolees to receive the supervision and assistance they need to avoid returning to the same lifestyle that put them in the criminal justice system in the first place.

Today, more prisons are being built to house those sentenced to prison. These will be staffed with counselors, teachers, guards, and professionals in the field of corrections. However, current statistics indicate that the planned increase in prison space cannot possibly catch up with the increasing crime rate. Therefore, Texas needs to consider alternatives.

For example, restitution centers or half-way houses for non-violent offenders have worked in other states. At these centers, inmates are released each day to go to work, then return in the evening. A portion of their earnings is used to pay court fines, make restitution to victims of their crimes, and pay the cost of the center.

Just as additional prison space is expensive, so are more judges, district attorneys, and parole and probation officers. Any cure for the problems faced by the Texas criminal justice system is expensive. But the costs of the rising crime rate that affects so many Texans is much higher.

Eighty percent of the inmates in Texas prisons are high school dropouts. A long-term solution to the crime rate and ills of the criminal justice system is to improve the Texas system of public education and develop better ways to keep students in school.

Meaningful educational reform is expensive. But, in the long run, such reform would mean fewer people requiring the enormous per capita expense of the criminal justice system, fewer individuals receiving public assistance, and more people contributing tax monies to lessen the costs for everyone.

Also, fewer people in the criminal justice system would allow the system to work as it is designed to work, reducing recidivism (those who return to prison). In this telelesson, Raymond Teske, professor of criminal justice at Sam Houston State University in Huntsville, examines the role of the TDCJ in rehabilitation and assesses how well the TDCJ currently functions under its handicaps.

Learning Objectives

Goal: The purpose of this lesson is to review the criminal justice system in Texas as a basis for evaluating proposals for improvements to the system.

Objectives:

1. Outline the steps in a criminal trial in Texas, including functions of juries, pretrial actions, sentencing, and the appellate process.

2. Describe the response in Texas to increases in crime rates and resultant overcrowding in the prisons.

3. Discuss suggestions proposed to make the criminal justice system in Texas more effective.

4. Review the roles and operational costs of the Texas Department of Criminal Justice and the Texas Board of Criminal Justice, and the effect of the case of *Ruiz v Estelle* on these agencies.

5. Explain the functions of parole, probation, community-based rehabilitation, and victim compensation in the criminal justice system in Texas.

Key Terms

Watch for these terms and pay particular attention to what each one means, as you follow the textbook and telelesson.

Grand jury
Trial jury
Indictment
True bill
No bill
Plaintiff
Defendant
Verdict
Nolo contendere

Plea bargain
Ruiz v Estelle
Texas Department of Criminal Justice (T.D.C.J.)
Probation
Parole
Board of Pardons and Paroles
Crime Victim Compensation Act

Textbook Reading Assignment

Jones, Ericson, Brown, and Trotter. *Practicing Texas Politics*, 8th edition. Chapter 8, "Law, Courts, and Justice," pp. 361-420, especially pp. 382-403 and 414-417.

Jones, Ericson, Brown, Trotter, and Lynch. *Practicing Texas Politics – A Brief Survey*, 4th edition. Chapter 8, "Law, Courts, and Justice," pp. 222- 261, especially pp. 238-261.

Note to students: You are responsible for only *one* of these reading assignments. It is your responsibility to know which book is used in your class.

Textbook Focus Points

Before you read the textbook assignment, review the following points to help focus your thoughts. After you complete the assignment, write your responses to reinforce what you have learned.

1. What are the functions of grand juries and trial juries?

2. What is the procedure for criminal trials in Texas? Describe pretrial actions, aspects of a trial in criminal cases, the verdict and sentence, and the appellate process in a criminal case.

3. What is the role of the Texas Department of Criminal Justice in the criminal justice system in Texas? What is the function of the Texas Board of Criminal Justice and the importance of the case of *Ruiz v Estelle* in the administration of justice in Texas?

4. How has Texas addressed the problems of prison overcrowding? What is the function of parole and probation within the criminal justice system and in easing the problems of prison overcrowding?

5. What are community-based rehabilitation programs? Explain their function within the criminal justice system.

6. What is the purpose of the Crime Victim Compensation Act?

7. What are the problems facing the criminal justice system in Texas? Discuss possible solutions to some of these problems.

Telelesson Interviewees

The following individuals will share their expertise in the telelesson:

Ron Chapman–State District Judge, Dallas County
Marshall Herklotz–Northern Regional Director, Texas Department of Criminal Justice
Allen Hightower–Member, Texas House of Representatives, Huntsville
John Holmes–District Attorney, Harris County
Edgar Ruiz–County Judge, Hidalgo County
Raymond Teske–Department of Criminal Justice, Sam Houston State University

Telelesson Focus Points

Before viewing the telelesson, read the following points to help focus your thoughts. After the presentation, write your responses to reinforce these important points.

1. In Texas, how have state government and jurors responded to the increase in crime? How have these responses affected problems in the criminal justice system?

2. How do the views of Harris County District Attorney John Holmes and State District Judge Ron Chapman differ on how to make the criminal justice system more effective?

3. How are the operational costs of the Texas Department of Criminal Justice defrayed?

4. What is the goal of the Texas Department of Criminal Justice, and how is this goal accomplished?

5. What do experts offer as the two-fold approach to improving the criminal justice system in Texas?

Recommended Reading

The following suggestions are not required unless your instructor assigns them. They are listed to let you know where you can find additional information on areas which interest you.

Atkinson, Jim. "Bail Bonding Can be Sleazy and Unfair—But It Works." *Texas Monthly* (September 1986): pp. 18, 19.

___. "To Plea or Not to Plea—The Question's Moot in El Paso." *Texas Monthly* (April 1986): pp. 18, 20.

Baird, Lester H. "Texas Prison Gangs." *Criminal Justice Today* (July 1986): pp. 12, 18, 22.

Brasfield, Philip. "Life and Death in the TDCJ." *Texas Observer* (January 29, 1988): pp. 22-23.

Crouch, Ben M. and James W. Marquart, *An Appeal to Justice: Litigated Reform of Texas Prisons.* Austin: University of Texas Press, 1989.

Getting Involved

This activity is not required unless your instructor assigns it. But it offers good suggestions to help you understand and become more involved in the political process.

> Visit with a probation or parole officer and discuss the advantages and disadvantages of probation and parole in Texas.

Self Test

After reading the assignment and watching the telelesson, you should be able to answer these questions. When you have completed the test, turn to the Answer Key to score your answers.

1. A group of citizens selected to determine if there is sufficient evidence to accuse a person of a crime is called a
   a. petit jury.
   b. trial jury.
   c. home jury.
   d. grand jury.

2. Juries which render verdicts in civil and criminal cases are known as
   a. trial juries.
   b. grand juries.
   c. magistrate juries.
   d. home juries.

3. Which jury requires a unanimous verdict?
   a. Grand jury
   b. Trial jury in a civil case
   c. Trial jury in a criminal case
   d. Hung jury

4. When the accused pleads guilty in return for the promise that the prosecution will seek a lighter sentence or will recommend probation, the attorneys in the case have engaged in
   a. corruption.
   b. plea bargaining.
   c. *nolo contendere.*
   d. parole.

5. In a trial of a criminal case, a judge may refuse to accept the verdict of the jury and
   a. pardon the accused.
   b. change the verdict.
   c. refer the case to a higher court.
   d. order a new trial.

6. In *Ruiz v Estelle*, U.S. District Court Judge William Wayne Justice
   a. condemned overcrowding in units of the then Texas Department of Corrections.
   b. closed the substandard facilities of the Texas Youth Commission.
   c. forced the legislature to allocate more funds for prison reforms.
   d. ruled that all persons charged with crimes must be released on bail pending trial.

7. Overcrowding in units of the Texas Department of Criminal Justice has caused
   a. more executions in order to make room for new prisoners.
   b. fewer convictions of persons charged with felony offenses.
   c. more good-time credit in order to allow early release of prisoners.
   d. shorter sentences for white-collar and non-violent crimes.

8. One way in which Texas has addressed the problems of prison overcrowding is to
   a. reduce the amount of good-time credit awarded inmates in the Texas Department of Criminal Justice.
   b. build several new prisons.
   c. decrease the use of probation and pre-trial release programs.
   d. greatly enlarge the number of parole and probation officers.

9. Parole and probation
   a. are designed to rehabilitate convicted criminals.
   b. were declared unconstitutional by the U.S. Supreme Court.
   c. are granted by the governor on the recommendation of the Board of Pardons and Paroles.
   d. are granted by the Board of Pardons and Paroles on the recommendation of the Governor's Council on Rehabilitation.

10. Which of the following is NOT an example of a community-based rehabilitation program?
   a. Confinement
   b. Compensation to victims of the crime
   c. Participation in community-service projects
   d. Serving in a community rehabilitation center

11. The purpose of the Crime Victim Compensation Act is to
   a. reward criminals who make restitution to victims of their crimes.
   b. provide a means for victims of crimes to recover lost wages and medical bills not covered by insurance.
   c. institute a means by which criminals pay for the cost of their trials and incarceration.
   d. reduce the number of criminals entering the Texas Department of Criminal Justice by requiring criminals to work for their victims.

12. Which of the following is NOT a problem facing Texas' criminal justice system?
   a. Increasing numbers of people entering the system
   b. Orders of federal courts which restrict what Texas can do
   c. Absence of land on which to build new prisons
   d. Lack of money to implement reforms

13. As the crime rate in Texas increased, juries in Texas
    a. sentenced criminals to longer prison terms.
    b. sentenced criminals to shorter prison terms.
    c. did not change the length of terms given to criminals.
    d. were not allowed to impose sentences.

14. The Harris County district attorney suggests that the criminal justice system in Texas can be improved by
    a. increased use of community rehabilitation programs.
    b. increased use of probation and restitution.
    c. harsher, more unpleasant experiences in the Texas Department of Criminal Justice for criminals.
    d. implementing the Roget approach to criminal justice.

15. Operational costs in the Texas Department of Criminal Justice are defrayed by
    a. early release of convicts.
    b. use of the Roget system.
    c. implementation of a crime district tax in Texas' four largest cities.
    d. prison industries which provide goods and services to other state agencies.

16. Which of the following is NOT a way in which the Texas Department of Criminal Justice meets its goal to rehabilitate inmates?
    a. Early release to keep state prisons at no more than 95% of capacity
    b. Vocational training programs
    c. High school diploma and college degree programs
    d. Alcohol and drug rehabilitation programs

17. Experts suggest that the key to solving the problems of Texas' rising crime rate and overcrowded prisons is to attack the underlying causes of crime, such as poverty, drug use, and illiteracy, and
   a. increase the number of state prisons.
   b. make punishments for criminals swift and sure.
   c. implement broader use of solitary confinement.
   d. sentence criminals to longer prison terms.

Answer Key

These are the correct answers with reference to the Learning Objectives, and to the source of the information: the Textbook Focus Points, Jones, *et al. Practicing Texas Politics* (Jones) or Jones, *et. al., Practicing Texas Politics — A Brief Survey* (Survey); the Study Guide Overview (Overview); and the Telelesson Focus Points. Page numbers are also given for the Textbook Focus Points. "KT" indicates questions with Key Terms defined.

Question	Answer	Learning Objective	Textbook Focus Point (page no.)	Telelesson Focus Point
1	D	1	1 (Jones, pp. 382-383; Survey, pp. 238-239)......KT	
2	A	1	1 (Jones, pp. 383-384; Survey, pp. 239-240)......KT	
3	C	1	2 (Jones, p. 388; Survey, pp. 243-244)	
4	B	1	2 (Jones, p. 387; Survey, p. 243)...............KT	
5	D	1	2 (Jones, p. 388; Survey, p. 244)	
6	A	4	3 (Jones, p. 391; Survey, p. 246)	
7	C	2	4 (Jones, pp. 391-393; Survey, pp. 246-248)	
8	B	2	4 (Jones, pp. 391-394; Survey, pp. 246-249)	
9	A	5	4 (Jones, pp. 395-397; Survey, pp. 250-253)	
10	A	5	5 (Jones, pp. 395-397; Survey, pp. 250-253)	
11	B	5	6 (Jones, p. 401; Survey, p. 257)...............KT	
12	C	3	7 (Jones, pp. 391-395; Survey, pp. 246-249)	
13	A	2		1
14	C	3		2
15	D	4		3
16	A	4		4
17	B	3		5

WARNING TO BE GIVEN BEFORE TAKING
ANY ORAL OR WRITTEN CONFESSION

(1) You have the right to remain silent and not make any statement at all and any statement you make may be used against you at your trial;

(2) Any statement you make may be used as evidence against you in court;

(3) You have the right to have a lawyer present to advise you prior to and during any questioning;

(4) If you are unable to employ a lawyer, you have the right to have a lawyer appointed to advise you prior to and during any questioning; and,

(5) You have the right to terminate the interview at any time.

LEGAL LIAISON DIVISION — DALLAS POLICE DEPARTMENT

POL-81646

Lesson 19

Rights of the Accused

Overview

The rights of a society and the rights of a person accused of a crime are always in tension. At the same time, we strongly believe that no innocent person should be punished. This lesson highlights the dynamic conflict between society and the accused, as we continue our study of the Bill of Rights. Here we focus on the procedural rights guaranteed to each of us if we are accused of a crime. As page 120 of the text says, "The emphasis on doing things by the rules, almost without regard to whether the decision itself is fair, is the hallmark of procedural due process."

Society in general supports the idea that the same procedures ought to be followed toward everyone, citizen and non-citizen alike, who is accused of a crime. But we usually don't claim these procedural rights—and we almost never realize how important they are—until or unless we are accused.

We also believe that no government can take away a person's life, liberty, or property without "due process of law," which is why due process is preserved in the Constitution and in Amendments Four through Eight. Some additional points important to our system of justice are the presumption that a person is innocent until proven guilty, and the belief that it is better for the guilty to go free than for one innocent person to be punished unjustly.

To illustrate some of the rights guaranteed in matters of procedure, we examine some landmark Supreme Court decisions:

Mapp v. Ohio (1961) applied the exclusionary rule, which determined what evidence was admissable in court and how it could legally be gathered, favoring the accused.

California v. Billy Greenwood (1988) also applied Amendment Four to the gathering of evidence, but expanded police authority.

Gideon v. Wainwright (1963) extended the Sixth Amendment guarantee of counsel to the states and to poor people.

Miranda v. Arizona (1966) incorporated Amendments Five and Six to guarantee that those accused can have counsel present during interrogation and that the accused have a right to "take the Fifth."

After *Gideon* and *Miranda* had expanded the rights of the accused, *New York v. Quarles* (1984) restricted these expanded rights by modifying the *Miranda* ruling in the interest of public safety.

The rights of the accused versus the rights of society to be safe and secure in our homes and on our streets is in a constant state of imbalance. But unless all of us can live under the assurance of our constitutional rights, none of us is either truly free or truly protected by the law—or from the law.

Learning Objectives

Goal: The purpose of "Rights of the Accused" is to explain the procedural rights guaranteed by the Bill of Rights that protect individuals accused of a crime and to describe the dynamic conflict between the rights of society and the rights of the accused.

Objectives:

1. Explain how each of these terms relate to the rights of the accused: writ of *habeas corpus;* due process; trial rights, pretrial rights, and limits on police conduct; the *Miranda* decision, including some exceptions; and the exclusionary rule.

2. Explain the effect of the following landmark cases on the rights of the accused: *Mapp v. Ohio, Gideon v. Wainwright, Miranda v. Arizona,* and *California v. Billy Greenwood.*

3. Assess the conflict in our society over capital punishment, and see how some states have resolved the conflict.

4. Describe the conflict in our society regarding protecting the rights of people accused of a crime versus protecting the rights of everyone else.

5. Show how the Fourth, Fifth, Sixth and Eighth Amendments affect the rights of the accused and protect that person's life, liberty, and property.

Key Terms

Watch for these terms and pay particular attention to what each one means, as you follow the textbook and telelesson.

Writ of *habeas corpus*	"Taking the Fifth" (TV)
Exclusionary rule	*Miranda* warning (TV)
Capital crimes (TV)	

Textbook Reading Assignment

Schmidt, Shelley, and Bardes. *American Government and Politics Today,* 1993-94 edition. Chapter 4, "Civil Liberties," pp. 102, 129-138.

Textbook Focus Points

Before you read the textbook assignment, review the following points to help focus your thoughts. After you complete the assignment, write out your responses to reinforce what you have learned.

1. What is a writ of *habeas corpus,* and how does it protect the rights of the accused?

2. What are some of the basic rights of criminal defendants with regard to trial rights, pre-trial rights, and limits on police conduct?

3. How did the verdict in the *Miranda* decision extend the rights of the accused?

4. What impact have recent Supreme Court rulings had on the *Miranda* decision?

5. What is the exclusionary rule, and how does it protect the rights of the accused?

6. What did Clarence Earl Gideon contribute to the rights of the accused?

7. What is the conflict over capital punishment, and how have some states resolved it?

Telelesson Interviewees

The following individuals share their expertise in the telelesson:

Mary Broderick–National Legal Aid and Defense Association
Reuben Greenberg–Chief of Police, Charleston, South Carolina

Fred Inbau–Professor Emeritus, Northwestern University Law School

Norman Kinne –Assistant District Attorney, Dallas, Texas

Peter Lesser–Criminal Defense Attorney, Dallas, Texas

John R. Schmidhauser–Professor of Political Science, University of Southern California

Telelesson Focus Points

Before viewing the telelesson, read over the following points to help focus your thoughts. After the presentation, write out your responses to help you remember these important points.

1. What conflict arises in our society regarding the rights of the accused, and how are these rights protected?

2. What protection does the Fourth Amendment provide against unreasonable search and seizure?

3. What legal concept did *Mapp v. Ohio* apply, and what effect has this had on the rights of the accused?

4. How did the *Billy Greenwood* case affect the application of the exclusionary rule?

5. How do the provisions of the Eighth Amendment protect the rights of the accused?

6. How does the verdict in the *Gideon* case affect the application of the Sixth Amendment?

7. How does the *Miranda* decision affect the Fifth Amendment provision regarding self-incrimination?

8. What are some exceptions to the *Miranda* ruling?

Recommended Reading

The following suggestions are not required unless your instructor assigns them. They are listed to let you know where you can find additional information on areas which interest you.

Jacoby, Ted. "Fighting Crime by the Rules." *Newsweek* 112 (July 18, 1988): p. 53.

Lewis, Anthony. *Gideon's Trumpet*. New York: Vintage, 1964.

Methvin, Eugene. "The Case of Common Sense vs. Miranda." *Reader's Digest* 131 (August 1987): pp. 96-100.

Sanders, Alain. "Lifting the Lid on Garbage." *Time* 131 (May 30, 1988): p. 54.

"Secrets of Trash." *Fortune* 117 (June 20, 1988): p. 119.

Uviller, H. Richard. " Does It Protect your Garbage?" *Nation* 247 (October 10, 1988): pp. 302-304.

Getting Involved

These activities are not required unless your instructor assigns them. But they offer good suggestions to help you understand and become more involved in the political process.

1. Note the "Getting Involved" section of your textbook at the end of Chapter 4.

2. In order to understand the impact of *Miranda v. Arizona* favoring the accused, talk with a senior or retired police officer and with a junior police officer. Ask them how arrest procedures have changed since the *Miranda* ruling. Do they favor or oppose the decision? Why?

Self Test

After reading the assignment and watching the telelesson, you should be able to answer these questions. When you have completed the test, turn to the Answer Key to score your answers.

1. "You should have the body" is the literal meaning of
   a. Writ of *mandamus*
   b. Writ of *certiorari*
   c. Writ of *habeas corpus*
   d. Exclusionary rule

2. Limits on conduct of police and prosecutors include no
   a. unreasonable or unwarranted searches or seizures.
   b. questioning of individuals until they are arrested.
   c. habeas corpus.
   d. breaking and entering for public safety.

3. In Miranda's appeal, his attorney argued that the police had never informed Miranda that he had the right to
   a. a writ of habeas corpus and the right to reasonable bail.
   b. remain silent and the right to be represented by counsel.
   c. no arrest except for probable cause and the right to appeal conviction.
   d. prompt arraignment and the right to confront all witnesses.

4. The Supreme Court under Chief Justice Warren Burger did not expand the *Miranda* ruling,
   a. but it did change the focus of the ruling.
   b. although it did provide counsel early in questioning.
   c. but instead somewhat reduced its scope and effectiveness.
   d. even though most civil rights groups wanted it to do so.

5. The exclusionary rule prohibits
   a. defendants from testifying in their own behalf.
   b. improperly obtained evidence from being used by prosecutors.
   c. use of evidence seized by means of a search warrant.
   d. defense counsel from having access to legally obtained evidence.

6. The heart of Gideon's petition to the Supreme Court lay in his notion that "to try a poor man for a felony without giving him a lawyer was to deprive him of
   a. the writ of *habeas corpus*."
   b. taking the Fifth."
   c. his Miranda rights."
   d. due process of law."

7. In 1972, the Supreme Court agreed that the death penalty, as applied in most states, was
   a. random and arbitrary.
   b. rare but fair.
   c. deserved but arbitrary.
   d. a necessary deterrent

8. In determining the guilt or innocence of a defendant, our society accepts the premise that it is better to
   a. follow the principle of "an eye for an eye."
   b. base justice on the code of the West.
   c. allow some guilty persons to go free than for one innocent person to be punished.
   d. punish one innocent person unjustly than for the guilty to escape punishment.

9. The Supreme Court's interpretation of the Fourth Amendment determines if
   a. individuals have been given a fair and legal trial.
   b. evidence has been gathered properly by the police.
   c. individuals have been put in jeopardy twice.
   d. sentences are cruel and unusual punishment.

10. The Supreme Court ruling in *Mapp v. Ohio* that the police had conducted an unreasonable search and seizure was an early application of the legal concept of
    a. writ of *habeas corpus*.
    b. "taking the Fifth."
    c. the *Miranda* doctrine.
    d. the exclusionary rule.

11. In the *Greenwood* case, the Supreme Court ruled that evidence obtained from the garbage or trash of a criminal suspect without a search warrant is legal because
    a. garbage is considered outside the bounds of an individual's home.
    b. garbage is not of value to anyone.
    c. search warrants can't be specific about the who, where, or why of garbage or trash.
    d. evidence found in a person's garbage can be destroyed easily.

12. The Eighth Amendment comes into play to protect the accused from
    a. unreasonable searches.
    b. double jeopardy.
    c. excessive bail.
    d. self-incrimination.

Rights of the Accused

13. The *Gideon* case concerned the application of the Sixth Amendment
    a. protection from unreasonable searches.
    b. guarantee of right to counsel.
    c. prohibition against excessive bail.
    d. protection from self-incrimination.

14. Which of the following provisions was NOT established in the *Miranda* case?
    a. The accused individual is entitled to an attorney before questioning.
    b. The accused individual must be advised of the constitutional right to remain silent.
    c. Any statement the accused makes may be used against that person.
    d. A defendant cannot be tried for the same crime twice.

15. The *New York v. Quarles* decision modified the *Miranda* ruling, shifting the balance to favor the rights of the
    a. public to be safe and secure, over the rights of the accused.
    b. accused to have a fair trial, over the rights of the public to be safe and secure.
    c. police to prosecute successfully, over the rights of the accused to receive a fair trial.
    d. defendant to have counsel, over the rights of the police to prosecute.

Short-Answer Question:
16. Where do you think the balance of rights is today, in favor of the accused or in favor of society? Why?

Answer Key

These are the correct answers with reference to the Learning Objectives, and to the source of the information: the Textbook Focus Points, Schmidt, *et al. American Government and Politics Today* (Schmidt), and the Telelesson Focus Points. Page numbers are also given for the Textbook Focus Points. "KT" indicates questions with Key Terms defined.

Question	Answer	Learning Objective	Textbook Focus Point (page no.)	Telelesson Focus Point
1	C	1	1 (Schmidt, p. 130)...........KT	
2	A	1	2 (Schmidt, p. 129)	
3	B	1	3 (Schmidt, p. 130)	
4	C	2	4 (Schmidt, p. 130)...........KT	
5	B	1	5 (Schmidt, p. 132)...........KT	
6	D	2	6 (Schmidt, p. 131)	
7	A	3	7 (Schmidt, p. 133)	
8	C	4		1
9	B	5		2
10	D	2	5 (Schmidt, p. 132)...........KT	3
11	A	2		4
12	C	5		5
13	B	2,5	6 (Schmidt, p. 131)	6
14	D	5	3 (Schmidt, p. 130)...........KT	7
15	A	1	4 (Schmidt, p. 132)	8

Short Answer:

16		4	2 (Schmidt, pp. 132-135)	1

The Supreme Court of Texas

Members of the court include: *Chief Justice Thomas Phillips (center, front); (from left to right) Justices Nathan Hecht, Eugene Cook, Raul Gonzalez, Franklin Spears, C.L. Ray, Oscar Mauzy, Jack Hightower, and LLoyd Doggett.*

Judicial Review

Overview

Judicial review means the right of a court to evaluate the action or lack of action on the part of legislative and executive officials or lower courts, to determine if it is in keeping with the U.S. Constitution or a state constitution. Any court exercises judicial review when it holds some action or inaction unconstitutional.

In a constitutional context, judicial review expresses the concept stated in *Marbury v Madison* the first time a law of Congress was held unconstitutional, that it is "the province and the duty of the judicial department to say what the law is." Under this doctrine, the U.S. Supreme Court and the highest state courts have assumed the power and responsibility to determine the constitutionality of acts of the legislative and executive branches of their respective jurisdictions.

But judicial review doesn't guarantee a single, definitive answer that will last forever. The U.S. Supreme Court exercised judicial review in 1896, in the case of *Plessy v Ferguson*, when it decided that the concept of "separate but equal" was constitutional and did not violate the equal protection clause of the U.S. Constitution. In the case of *Brown v Board of Education*, decided fifty-eight years later, the same court held that "separate but equal" was *not* constitutional and *did* violate the equal protection clause; it was also exercising judicial review.

When the U.S. Supreme Court ruled that states could not collect a poll tax, it exercised judicial review over actions by states that it found conflicted with the U.S. Constitution. When the Supreme Court declared that the application of the death penalty violated the U.S. Constitution and later ruled that revised state laws imposing the death penalty *were* constitutional, it was exercising judicial review in both instances.

But judicial review is not limited to the U.S. Supreme Court. Virtually any court can exercise judicial review. In the telelesson we examine judicial review as it affects Texas, from the perspective of three different courts' actions: the U.S. Supreme Court decisions concerning application of the death penalty, decisions of a U.S. District Court regarding the operation of the Texas Department of Criminal Justice, and a case in which the Texas Supreme Court found the method Texas uses to fund its public schools to be unconstitutional.

Learning Objectives

Goal: The purpose of this lesson is to provide both historical and current examples as the basis for illustrating the concept of judicial review.

Objectives:

1. Define the concept of judicial review as it involves the various levels of federal and state government.

2. Review the significance of three historical examples of judicial review: *Marbury v Madison, Plessy v Ferguson,* and *Brown v Board of Education.*

3. Describe the facts associated with three recent examples of judicial review—*Branch v Texas, Ruiz v Estelle,* and *Edgewood I.S.D. v Kirby*—and the resultant effect on government, politics, and the judicial system in Texas.

4. Discuss new issues expected to reach the courts in the near future.

Key Terms

Watch for these terms and pay particular attention to what each one means, as you follow the textbook and telelesson.

Judicial review   *Ruiz v Estelle*
Marbury v Madison   *Edgewood I.S.D. v Kirby*
Branch v Texas

Textbook Reading Assignment

There is no textbook reading assignment for this lesson; however, you are responsible for the information contained in the "Overview." There will be Overview focus points, self-test questions, and questions on your unit examination on material found in the "Overview."

Overview Focus Points

Before you read the assignment, review the following points to help focus your thoughts. After you complete the assignment, write your responses to reinforce what you have learned.

1. What is judicial review? What is the significance of *Marbury v Madison* in a study of judicial review?

2. What are three examples of judicial review cited in the Overview?

3. What courts can exercise judicial review?

Telelesson Interviewees

The following individuals will share their expertise in the telelesson:

Karyne Conley–Member, Texas House of Representatives, San Antonio
Brian Dille–Department of Government, Odessa College
John Forshee–Dallas County Community College

Telelesson Focus Points

Before viewing the telelesson, read the following points to help focus your thoughts. After the presentation, write your responses to help you remember these important points.

1. What were the facts in *Branch v Texas*, and how is this case an example of judicial review? How did the results of this case affect the government, politics, and judicial system of Texas?

2. What were the facts in *Ruiz v Estelle*, and how is it an example of judicial review? How did the results of this case affect the government, politics, and judicial system of Texas?

3. What were the facts in *Edgewood I.S.D. v Kirby*, and how is it an example of judicial review? How did the results of this case affect the government, politics, and judicial system of Texas?

4. In the next few years, what new issues will come before the courts?

Recommended Reading

The following suggestions are not required unless your instructor assigns them. They are listed to let you know where you can find additional information on areas which interest you.

Beal, Ron. "The Scope of Judicial Review of Agency Rulemaking: The Interrelationship of Legislating and Rulemaking in Texas." *Baylor Law Review* 39 (Spring 1986): pp. 253-289.

Brasfield, Phillip. "Life and Death in TDC." *Texas Observer* (January 29, 1988): pp. 22-23.

Dilulio, John J., Jr., *Governing Prisons: A Comparative Study of Correctional Management.* New York: Free Press, 1987.

Johnson, Amy. "Texas Faces Up to Promises." *Texas Lawyer* (March 2, 1987): p. 6.

LaMarche, Gara; Arthur Eads; and Dave Denison. "On Capital Punishment." *Texas Observer* (June 17, 1988): pp. 10-13.

Martin, Steve, Jr., *et al.* "On Prison Construction." *Texas Observer* (September 2, 1988): pp. 6-10.

Sullivan, Charles. "The Backlash That Failed." *Texas Observer* (July 12, 1986): pp. 6-8.

Getting Involved

This activity is not required unless your instructor assigns it. But it offers good suggestions to help you understand and become more involved in the political process.

> In the next few years there will be judgments from the U.S. Supreme Court, Texas Supreme Court, and Texas Court of Criminal Appeals concerning school funding, election of state district court judges, right-to-life and freedom-of-choice decisions, the death penalty, and other issues. As you read the daily newspaper and watch television news, note these decisions and their effect on your daily life.

Self Test

After reading the assignment and watching the telelesson, you should be able to answer these questions. When you have completed the test, turn to the Answer Key to score your answers.

1. The right of a court to review acts of members of the legislative and executive branch is called
   a. *nolo contendere.*
   b. indictment.
   c. separation of powers.
   d. judicial review.

2. The first case in which the U.S. Supreme Court declared an act of the U.S. Congress unconstitutional was
   a. *Gibons v Ogden.*
   b. *Marbury v Madison.*
   c. *Pettus v Bland.*
   d. *Plessy v Ferguson.*

3. The U.S. Supreme Court exercised judicial review over state actions dealing with separate but equal facilities in *Plessy v Ferguson* and
   a. *Smith v Allwright.*
   b. *Brown v Board of Education.*
   c. *Harper v Virginia State Board of Elections.*
   d. *Byrd v Jordan.*

4. Any court may exercise judicial review, but it is most commonly exercised by the U.S. Supreme Court and _____ in their respective jurisdictions.
   a. federal district courts.
   b. international courts of justice.
   c. the highest state courts.
   d. federal district courts **and** the highest state courts

5. In death penalty cases, the court which exercised judicial review was the
   a. U.S. District Court.
   b. Texas Court of Criminal Appeals.
   c. Supreme Court of Texas.
   d. U.S. Supreme Court.

6. Since the Court declared the death penalty unconstitutional, Texas has
   a. not executed any prisoners.
   b. not written another capital punishment statute.
   c. written a new capital punishment statute, but has not executed any prisoners.
   d. written a new capital punishment statute and executed more prisoners than any other state.

7. In *Ruiz v Estelle*, the court which exercised judicial review was the
   a. U.S. District Court.
   b. U.S. Supreme Court.
   c. Texas Court of Criminal Appeals.
   d. Supreme Court of Texas.

8. A result of the court's decision in *Ruiz v Estelle* was
   a. a reduction in the crime rate.
   b. an appeal to the U.S. Supreme Court.
   c. the state building more prisons.
   d. the resignation of the governor and lieutenant governor.

9. In the school funding case, *Edgewood v Kirby*, judicial review was exercised by the
   a. Supreme Court of Texas.
   b. Texas Court of Appeals.
   c. U.S. Court of Appeals.
   d. U.S. Court of Claims.

10. At issue in *Edgewood v Kirby* was
    a. integration of school facilities in southeast Texas.
    b. equal educational opportunity without regard to the wealth of the district.
    c. constitutionality of the no-pass, no-play provisions of HB 72.
    d. federal funds for pre-kindergarten programs.

11. One of the major issues to be decided by the courts in the next few years will involve
    a. death-penalty issues.
    b. privacy.
    c. freedom from religion.
    d. censorship.

Answer Key

These are the correct answers with reference to the Learning Objectives, and to the source of the information: the Textbook Focus Points, Jones, *et al. Practicing Texas Politics* (Jones) or Jones, *et. al., Practicing Texas Politics — A Brief Survey* (Survey); the Study Guide Overview (Overview); and the Telelesson Focus Points. Page numbers are also given for the Textbook Focus Points. "KT" indicates questions with Key Terms defined.

Question	Answer	Learning Objective	Textbook Focus Point (page no.)	Telelesson Focus Point
1	D	1	1(Overview)	KT
2	B	2	1(Overview)	KT
3	B	2	2(Overview)	
4	D	1	3(Overview)	
5	D	3	3(Overview)	
6	D	3		1
7	A	3		2
8	C	3		2
9	A	3		3
10	B	3		3
11	B	4		4

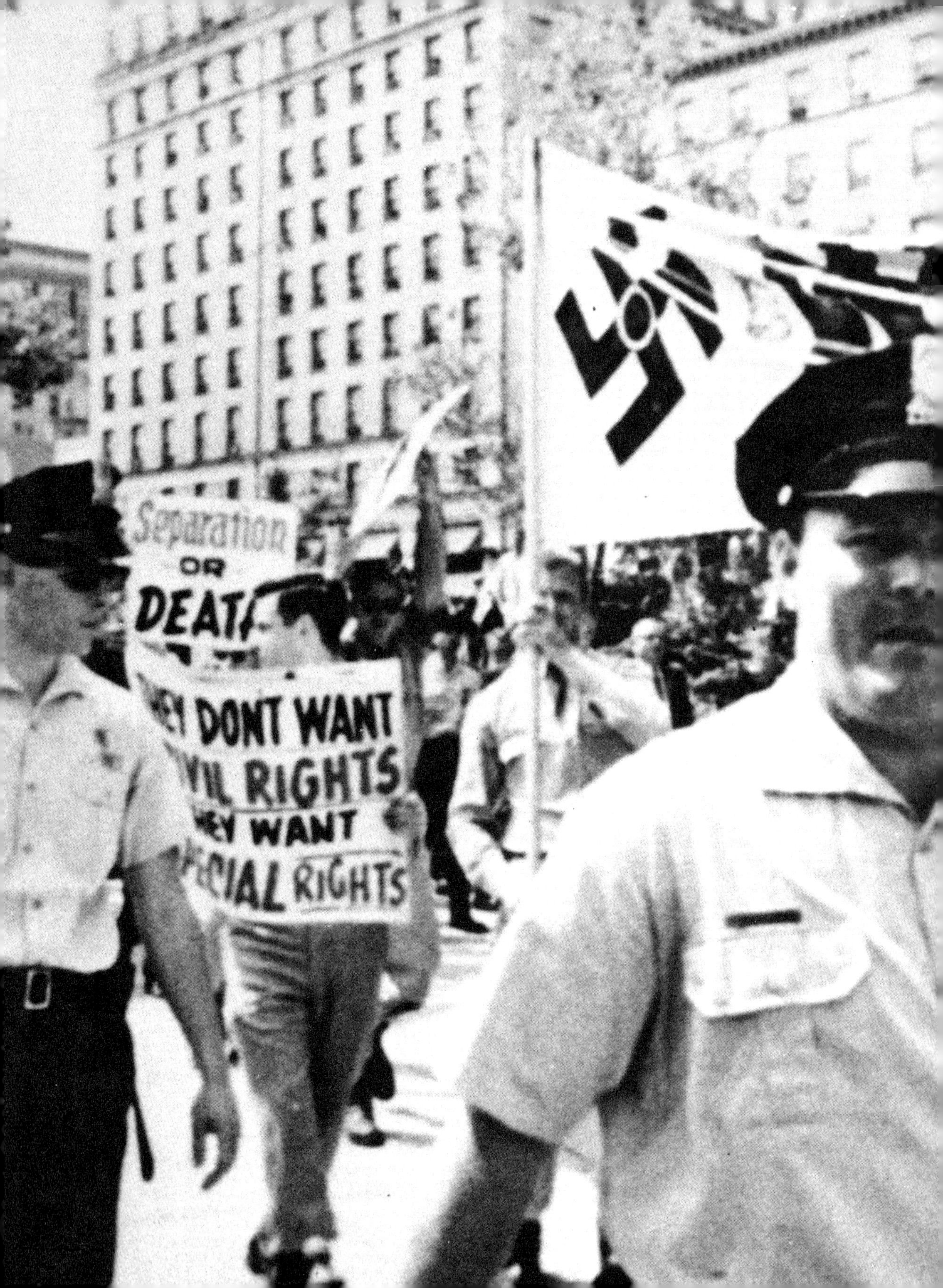

Separation
OR
DONT WANT
RIGHTS
WANT
RIGHTS

Lesson 21

Individual Rights

Overview

This lesson is one of three lessons dealing specifically with the U.S. Bill of Rights. In it we examine why these first ten amendments were proposed and ratified. Then we look at the Fourteenth Amendment and how it has been used to apply most of the Bill of Rights to the states. Finally, we investigate the role of the U.S. Supreme Court in interpreting the Constitution with all of its amendments. Another lesson focuses on the First Amendment freedoms. Yet another lesson highlights the rights guaranteed by the Bill of Rights to a person accused of a crime.

By the time the U.S. Bill of Rights was ratified on December 15, 1791, many states already had their own "bill of rights" in place to protect their citizens from abuse by the state. Therefore, the accepted view was that the national amendments applied only to the national government, a view which the Supreme Court confirmed in 1833 with its decision in *Barron v. Baltimore.*

Thirty-five years later the Fourteenth Amendment placed certain restrictions on the states in order to protect the rights of individuals throughout the nation. But in 1873 the Slaughter-House Cases established dual citizenship, determining that an individual is a citizen both of the nation and of the state in which he or she resides. Then the case of *Gitlow v. New York* began the slow, selective incorporation of the Bill of Rights protection to the states. Several recent and highly emotional cases, dealing with birth control and drug testing, have furthered this incorporation process.

We see how this all works as we talk with people from Skokie, Illinois. They wanted to deny the freedom of speech and assembly to an individual who was an avowed member of the American Nazi Party,

---

while many citizens of Skokie were survivors of concentration camps in Nazi Germany. Cases like these evoke strong emotions; the Supreme Court, in its role as interpreter of the Constitution, must separate public emotion from guaranteed freedoms. The idea that the majority rules is a strong one, and it prevails in the legislative branch. But the courts protect the minority.

Some rights protected by the Bill of Rights are very explicit, where others are more implied. Therefore, we must remember that our rights as individuals are guaranteed by the Constitution *as interpreted* by the Supreme Court of the United States.

Learning Objectives

Goal: The purpose of "Individual Rights" is to demonstrate that the rights of individuals are guaranteed by the U.S. Constitution *as interpreted* by the U.S. Supreme Court.

Objectives:

1. Outline the historical basis for the Bill of Rights, including the people whom it protects and its effect on their daily lives.

2. Explain how the Fourteenth Amendment protects individual rights.

3. Describe how the incorporation theory, especially the "equal protection" and "due process" clauses, affects the application of the Bill of Rights to the states.

4. Illustrate how the Bill of Rights applies to the states with regard to the rights to privacy, gun control, and peaceable assembly.

5. Contrast the roles which constitutional principle and popular emotion play in interpreting the Bill of Rights.

6. Explain the pivotal role of the Supreme Court in balancing individual rights with community rights, using the 1833 Supreme Court decision of *Barron v. Baltimore* as an example.

7. Explain the incident in Skokie, Illinois, as a test of the protection of free speech and right to assemble.

Key Terms

Watch for these terms and pay particular attention to what each one means, as you follow the textbook and telelesson.

Bill of Rights   **Incorporation theory**
Dual citizenship   **Euthanasia**

Textbook Reading Assignment

Schmidt, Shelley, and Bardes. *American Government and Politics Today,* 1993-94 edition. Chapter 4, "Civil Liberties," pp. 103-106, 123-128.

Textbook Focus Points

Before you read the textbook assignment, review the following points to help focus your thoughts. After you complete the assignment, write out your responses to reinforce what you have learned.

1. What is the Bill of Rights, and whom does it protect?

2. How has the Bill of Rights affected your life?

3. How does the Fourteenth Amendment help protect individual rights?

4. What is the incorporation theory, and how has it affected the application of the Bill of Rights to the states?

5. How may states restrict the First Amendment's guarantee of peaceable assembly?

6. On what is the right of privacy based, and to which current issues does it apply?

Telelesson Interviewees

The following individuals will share their expertise in the telelesson:

Erna Gans–Resident of Skokie, Illinois
David Goldberger–Former ACLU Attorney in Skokie, Illinois, Case
Barbara Jordan–Attorney and Professor, LBJ School of Public Affairs, University of Texas, Austin
Lawrence Mann–Attorney for the Railroad Labor Executive Association
Jack Mason–Former Chief Counsel, Federal Railroad Commission
John R. Schmidhauser–Professor of Political Science, University of Southern California
Harvey Schwartz–Former City Attorney for Skokie, Illinois

Telelesson Focus Points

Before viewing the telelesson, read over the following points to help focus your thoughts. After the presentation, write out your responses to help you remember these important points.

1. How are conflicts between constitutional principle and popular emotion resolved?

2. How did the 1833 Supreme Court decision of *Barron v. Baltimore* affect individual rights?

3. How has the Fourteenth Amendment affected individual rights?

4. How does "selective incorporation" relate to the Fourteenth Amendment's "equal protection" and "due process" clauses, and to the Bill of Rights?

5. How have gun-control laws been interpreted in light of the incorporation theory?

6. How did the incident in Skokie, Illinois, test the protection of the rights to free speech and peaceable assembly?

7. How does the Fourth Amendment apply to the right of privacy, and how does this affect drug testing?

Recommended Reading

The following suggestions are not required unless your instructor assigns them. They are listed to let you know where you can find additional information on areas which interest you.

Abraham, Henry J. *Freedom and the Court*. New York: Oxford University Press, 1982.

Hamlin, David. "Swastikas and Survivors: Inside the Skokie Free Speech Case." *The Civil Liberties Review* (March-April 1978).

"The High Cost of Free Speech: ACLU Defense of Nazi Demonstrators in Skokie." *Time* 111 (June 26, 1978): p. 63.

"The High Court Weighs Drug Tests." *Newsweek* 113 (April 3, 1989): p. 8.

Jacoby, Tamar. "Drug Testing on the Dock: Are Safety and Privacy Incompatible?" *Newsweek* 66 (November 14, 1988): p. 66.

Getting Involved

These activities are not required unless your instructor assigns them. But they offer good suggestions to help you understand and become more involved in the political process.

1. Abortion is a very controversial issue, evoking strong emotions from both sides. Set aside your personal beliefs and biases for the moment. Then research the pros and cons for each side, and write a brief essay on what you believe Supreme Court decisions should be on abortion issues and what constitutional basis you use for reaching your decision.

2. Mandatory drug testing is another very emotional issue. Research the topic, then decide which side you support and why. Write a few paragraphs outlining the factors in your decision and how you support your position constitutionally.

Self Test

After reading the assignment and watching the telelesson, you should be able to answer these questions. When you have completed the test, turn to the Answer Key to score your answers.

1. The first ten amendments to the U.S. Constitution, which contain a listing of the rights a person enjoys and which government cannot infringe upon, are called the
    a. writ of *habeas corpus.*
    b. Bill of Rights.
    c. positive law.
    d. incorporation theory.

2. As originally presented in the Constitution, the Bill of Rights
    a. limited the power of the national, not the state, government.
    b. protected citizens from all forms of government.
    c. protected citizens from both national and state governments.
    d. limited only the power of state governments.

3. It was not until the Fourteenth Amendment was ratified in 1868 that our Constitution explicitly
    a. dealt with the issue of slavery.
    b. addressed civil liberties.
    c. gave blacks the right to vote.
    d. guaranteed everyone due process of the law.

4. The Bill of Rights originally limited only the power of the national government but, through the years, most limitations have been applied to state governments through
    a. the *writ of habeas corpus.*
    b. dual-citizenship rulings.
    c. the selective incorporation theory.
    d. positive law.

5. The right of individuals to assemble and protest in public places may be DENIED when
   a. communists are involved.
   b. the Nazi Party is involved.
   c. government opposition is expected.
   d. matters of public safety are at issue.

6. The right to privacy is based on the
   a. concept that all men are created equal.
   b. rights set forth in Article I, Sections 9 and 10.
   c. concept that the Constitution's lack of a specific mention of the right to privacy does not mean that this right is denied.
   d. Twenty-seventh Amendment, which stipulates that all people have certain rights over which the federal government has no authority.

7. Public sentiment is separated from guaranteed freedoms through interpretation of the U.S. Constitution and Bill of Rights by the
   a. president.
   b. Supreme Court.
   c. attorney general.
   d. Congress.

8. The Supreme Court, in deciding *Barron v. Baltimore,*
   a. recognized a dual system of rights.
   b. reinforced the supremacy clause.
   c. made the judicial branch equal with the legislative and executive branches.
   d. initiated the "national commerce" clause.

9. On the basis of the Fourteenth Amendment, the U.S. Supreme Court protected individual rights by placing certain restraints on the
   a. president.
   b. states.
   c. Congress.
   d. bureaucracy.

10. In 1925, the Supreme Court's decision in *Gitlow v. New York* applied the Fourteenth Amendment to
    a. criminal cases.
    b. former slaves.
    c. the states.
    d. the federal government.

11. Some constitutional scholars argue that the Second Amendment does not guarantee an individual the right to bear arms without restriction, because the "right of the people" has been interpreted as a
    a. regional right, for the national militia or armed forces.
    b. state's right, for a state militia or national guard.
    c. collective right, for a group, not individuals.
    d. local right, at the discretion of local governments.

12. The Supreme Court, in deciding the *Skokie* case, was forced to
    a. choose the importance of freedom of speech over freedom to assemble.
    b. defend the statutes of a state government over the statutes of a local government.
    c. divide the issues of popular sentiment from the issues of unpopular sentiment.
    d. separate a constitutional right from a public emotion.

13. Those who oppose mandatory drug testing in the workplace claim that such testing
    a. would infringe on a fundamental constitutional right.
    b. would be a costly process and discriminate against people at lower economic levels.
    c. is an emotional issue that should be left to employers.
    d. is an issue which will police itself and should not be mandatory.

Short-Answer Question:

14. If you had been a judge serving on the court deciding the *Skokie* case, would you have ruled in favor of Frank Collin and the American Nazi Party, or in favor of the citizens of Skokie? On what constitutional point would you have based your decision?

Answer Key

These are the correct answers with reference to the Learning Objectives, and to the source of the information: the Textbook Focus Points, Schmidt, *et al. American Government and Politics Today* (Schmidt), and the Telelesson Focus Points. Page numbers are also given for the Textbook Focus Points. "KT" indicates questions with Key Terms defined.

Question	Answer	Learning Objective	Textbook Focus Point (page no.)	Telelesson Focus Point
1	B	1	1 (Schmidt, p. 103) ....KT	
2	A	1	2 (Schmidt, p. 104) ....KT	
3	D	2	3 (Schmidt, p. 104)	
4	C	3	4 (Schmidt, p. 105) ....KT	
5	D	4	5 (Schmidt, p. 124)	
6	C	4	6 (Schmidt, p. 125)	
7	B	5		1
8	A	6		2
9	B	2		3
10	C	3		4
11	C	4		5
12	D	7		6
13	A	4		7

Short Answer:

14		7	4,5 (Schmidt, p. 123-124)	6

JOINT ELECTION (ELECCION CONJUNTA)

JOINT ELECTION (ELECCION CONJUNTA)

CITY OF GARLAND (CIUDAD DE GARLAND)
CITY OF CARROLLTON (CIUDAD DE CARROLLTON)
CITY OF FARMERS BRANCH (CIUDAD DE FARMERS BRANCH)
DALLAS INDEPENDENT SCHOOL DISTRICT
(DISTRITO ESCOLAR INDEPENDIENTE DE DALLAS)
RICHARDSON INDEPENDENT SCHOOL DISTRICT
(DISTRITO ESCOLAR INDEPENDIENTE DE RICHARDSON)
DALLAS COUNTY COMMUNITY COLLEGE DISTRICT
(DISTRITO DE COLEGIO DE CONDADO DE DALLAS)

MAY 5, 1990 (5 DE MAYO DE 1990)

OFFICIAL BALLOT (BOLETA OFICIAL)

INSTRUCTIONS FOR PUNCH CARD VOTING

PLEASE READ ALL THE FOLLOWING INSTRUCTIONS BEFORE PROCEEDING TO VOTE

1. Without removing the stub, insert the ballot card in the voting device with the numbers showing. Hook the two holes at the top of the card over the two red posts at the top of the device.

2. Punch a hole in the space provided beside each candidate/proposition of your choice. Use only the punch device provided; never use pen or pencil.

3. WRITE-IN VOTING: If you wish to cast a write-in vote, request a write-in envelope and instructions from the precinct election judge. Do not write-in candidates or office titles in this booklet.

4. If you make a mistake or damage the ballot, return it to the election official and get another. You may not receive more than three ballots.

5. This is a joint election ballot for the political jurisdictions listed at the top of this page. Based on your residence, you are entitled to vote for those candidates/propositions listed on the following pages.

VOTE ALL PAGES

INSTRUCCIONES PARA VOTAR CON BOLETA ELECTRONICA

FAVOR DE LEER TODAS SIGUIENTES INSTRUCCIONES ANTES DE EMPEZAR A VOTAR

1. SIN QUITAR EL TALON, META LA TARJETA EN EL APARATO DE VOTACION CON LOS NUMEROS PARA ARRIBA. COLOQUE LOS DOS AGUJEROS A LA CABEZA DE LA TARJETA SOBRE LOS DOS POSTES ROJOS A LA CABEZA DEL APARATO.

2. HAGA UN AGUJERO EN EL ESPACIO PROVISTO AL LADO DE CADA CANDIDATO O PROPOSICION DE SU PREFERENCIA. USE SOLAMENTE EL PUNSON PROVISTO; NUNCA USE LA PLUMA O EL LAPIZ.

3. VOTANDO POR INSERCION ESCRITA: SI USTED VOTA EN AUSENCIA, PIDA UN SOBRE PARA BOLETAS VOTADOS EN AUSENCIA Y LOS INSTRUCCIONES DEL JUEZ ELECTORAL DEL PRECINTO. NO ESCRIBA LOS NOMBRES DE CANDIDATOS O TITULOS DE PUESTOS OFICIALES EN ESTE LIBRETIN.

4. SI USTED SE EQUIVOCA O SI DANA LA BOLETA, DEVUELVALA AL OFICIAL ELECTORAL Y OBTENGA OTRA. NO PUEDE RECIBIR MAS DE TRES BOLETAS.

5. ESTA ES UNA BOLETA PARA LA ELECCION CONJUNTA PARA LAS JURISDICCIONES POLITICAS NOMBRADAS A LA CABEZA DE ESTA PAGINA. SEGUN LA REGION DONDE RESIDE USTED ESTARA PERMITIDO VOTAR POR ESOS CANDIDATOS/PROPOSICIONES LISTADAS EN LAS SIGUIENTES PAGINAS.

VOTO TODAS LAS PAGINAS ➡

Lesson 22

Expansion of Voting Rights

Overview

Government by consent—In democratic societies we, the governed, use free elections as the primary way we choose our officeholders. Ideally, these elections counteract the ability of a few individuals or groups to control the lives of many. But this political system works best when choices are made by an informed, caring, and knowledgeable electorate. In the United States, we consent to be governed through actively taking part in the political process by voting, or we tacitly consent to government actions by not voting.

Why vote? Elections are seldom determined by one vote, so what difference does it make? The fundamental reason people vote is that we have been taught that it is our duty as citizens. Even though our one vote will almost never affect the outcome of an election, it is important that we take part. The participation of individual citizens is important to our political system and to our own development.

In Texas, universal suffrage—the right of every adult citizen to vote—has existed only for the past quarter century. Before that, a poll tax, which was a fee paid to register to vote; a property qualification for voting in bond elections; and the "white primary," allowing only Caucasians to vote, excluded significant numbers of people from voting. Today, voting rights in Texas have been greatly expanded through the adoption of the Fifteenth, Nineteenth, Twenty-fourth, and Twenty-sixth Amendments to the U. S. Constitution; the Voting Rights Acts; and court decisions like *Harper v Virginia State Board of Elections, Smith v Allwright,* and *Hill v Stone.*

At the same time, in Texas as in many other states, the level of voter participation is amazingly low. Yet voting is a precious freedom—a right deeply appreciated as demonstrated by the huge percentage of eligible voters turning out for free elections in eastern European countries, as they regain this privilege they had lost for so long.

Elections, and thus participation by individual voters, are crucial to the ongoing success of the U.S. political system. Voters certainly influence public policy, because elections confer legitimacy on winners. And participation is important, because the success of our system of government depends on significant numbers of voters making informed choices.

Learning Objectives

Goal: The purpose of this lesson is to review the evolution of voting rights in the United States and in Texas.

Objectives:

1. Describe the changes in federal and state laws which led to democratization of the ballot in Texas.

2. Evaluate the fairness of elections today in Texas, including voting districts, voter qualifications, and voter registration procedures.

3. Discuss the effects on suffrage in Texas of uniform voting rights across the fifty states and expansion of voting rights to virtually all citizens who are 18 years of age and older .

4. Assess the reasons why persons choose to vote or not to vote.

Key Terms

Watch for these terms and pay particular attention to what each one means, as you follow the textbook and telelesson.

Universal suffrage   **Poll tax**
White primary   **Voter registration**

Textbook Reading Assignment

Jones, Ericson, Brown, and Trotter. *Practicing Texas Politics*, 8th edition. Chapter 4, "The Politics of Elections and Parties," pp. 134-198, especially pp. 137-144.

Jones, Ericson, Brown, Trotter, and Lynch. *Practicing Texas Politics – A Brief Survey*, 4th Edition. Chapter 4, "The Politics of Elections and Parties," pp. 83-123, especially, pp. 84-88.

Note to students: You are responsible for only *one* of the books listed above. It is your responsibility to know which book is used in your class.

Textbook Focus Points

Before you read the textbook assignment, review the following points to help focus your thoughts. After you complete the assignment, write your responses to reinforce what you have learned.

1. How have elimination of the poll tax and the white primary contributed to the democratization of the ballot? How have the Voting Rights Act of 1965, and the Fifteenth, Nineteenth, Twenty-fourth, and Twenty-sixth Amendments to the U. S. Constitution, contributed to the democratization of the ballot?

2. What are the qualifications to vote in Texas? Who cannot vote even though they meet the state's qualifications?

3. How can people become registered to vote in Texas?

4. What are two trends in suffrage in Texas?

5. Why do individuals choose to vote or not to vote?

Telelesson Interviewees

The following individuals will share their expertise in the telelesson:

Scott Bennett–Columnist, *Dallas Morning News*
Eddie Cavazos–Member, Texas House of Representatives, Corpus Christi
Wilhelmina Delco–Member, Texas House of Representatives, Austin
Brian Dille–Department of Government, Odessa College
William Lawson–Pastor, Wheeler Avenue Baptist Church, Houston
Jim Mattox–Former Attorney General of Texas
Carlos Truan–Member, Texas Senate, Corpus Christi

Telelesson Focus Points

Before viewing the telelesson, read the following points to help focus your thoughts. After the presentation, write your responses to help you remember these important points.

1. How did Texas prohibit blacks from participating in the election process after the adoption of the Fifteenth Amendment to the U.S. Constitution?

2. How fair are elections today?

3. What was the importance of the Voting Rights Act of 1975 in expanding voter participation in Texas?

4. How will the increase in the African-American and Hispanic populations in Texas affect voting and politics?

Recommended Reading

The following suggestions are not required unless your instructor assigns them. They are listed to let you know where you can find additional information on areas which interest you.

Caro, Robert A. *The Path to Power.* Vol. 1 of *The Years of Lyndon Johnson.* New York: Alfred A. Knopf, 1982.

Citizens at Last! The Women's Suffrage Movement in Texas. Austin: Alice C. Temple, 1987.

Cook, Alison. "Vote for Me, Por Favor. Now Let's Eat." *Texas Monthly* (September 1986): pp. 136-138, 185-186, 188-191.

Davidson, Chandler, ed. *Minority Vote Dilution.* Washington, D.C.: Howard University Press, 1984.

"Hispanics in Texas: A Growing Political Force." *Hispanic Monitor* (April 1984): pp. 1-6.

Shockley, John. *Chicano Revolt in a Texas Town.* Notre Dame, Ind.: University of Notre Dame Press, 1974.

Getting Involved

This activity is not required unless your instructor assigns it. But it offers good suggestions to help you understand and become more involved in the political process.

Register to vote. For each election follow the candidates and/or issues. Vote.

Self Test

After reading the assignment and watching the telelesson, you should be able to answer these questions. When you have completed the test, turn to the Answer Key to score your answers.

1. The right of virtually all adults to vote is called
   a. universal suffrage.
   b. boundless voting.
   c. engrossment.
   d. crossover voting.

2. The white primary restricted voting in
   a. Republican primaries.
   b. Democratic primaries.
   c. general elections.
   d. bond elections.

3. The poll tax was declared unconstitutional by
   a. the Fifteenth Amendment to the Texas Constitution.
   b. the Civil Rights Act of 1964.
   c. *Smith v Allwright.*
   d. *Harper v Virginia State Board of Elections.*

4. The Nineteenth Amendment to the U.S. Constitution granted the right to vote to
   a. women.
   b. African-American males.
   c. eighteen year olds.
   d. non-citizens.

5. To be eligible to vote in Texas, an individual must have
   a. lived in Texas one year.
   b. reached eighteen years of age.
   c. lived in a Texas county for sixty days.
   d. lived in a Texas voting precinct for thirty days.

---

6. Even though you meet all other qualifications to vote in Texas, you are prohibited from voting if you are
   a. an election official.
   b. a college student.
   c. a recently convicted felon.
   d. in a common-law marriage.

7. Voter registration in Texas is administered by the
   a. secretary of state.
   b. county voting registrar.
   c. national elections administrator.
   d. municipal elector.

8. A major trend in suffrage is
   a. significantly more people voting.
   b. tightening of registration requirements.
   c. uniformity of voting policies among the fifty states.
   d. lack of uniformity of voting policies among the fifty states.

9. The most important factor in determining if an individual will vote is
   a. gender.
   b. race.
   c. level of income.
   d. education.

10. Since 1968, the percentage of Texans casting ballots in presidential elections has (Jones, 8th ed.)
    a. increased dramatically.
    b. increased somewhat.
    c. decreased dramatically.
    d. remained almost constant.

11. After the adoption of the Fifteenth Amendment to the U. S. Constitution, Texas was able to exclude African-Americans from voting by using the white primary and
    a. literacy test.
    b. character test.
    c. poll tax.
    d. property tax.

12. Elections in Texas today are considered unfair by many because
    a. legal aliens are excluded from voting.
    b. those age eighteen to twenty-one are excluded from voting.
    c. the Civil Rights Act of 1964 has never been applied to Texas.
    d. legislative and congressional districts are not truly representative of the electorate.

13. Voter registration and elections in Texas are supervised by the U.S. Department of Justice under provisions of the
    a. Voting Rights Act of 1975.
    b. Civil Rights Act of 1975.
    c. Thirteenth, Fourteenth, Fifteenth, and Twenty-second Amendments to the U. S. Constitution.
    d. U.S. Supreme Court decision in *Dennison v Kartum*.

Short-Answer Question:
14. Based on readings in the textbook and "Overview," your reading of newspapers, and viewing the video, describe at least two ways in which the increase in the African-American and Hispanic populations will affect the politics of Texas.

Answer Key

These are the correct answers with reference to the Learning Objectives, and to the source of the information: the Textbook Focus Points, Jones, *et al. Practicing Texas Politics* (Jones) or Jones, *et. al., Practicing Texas Politics — A Brief Survey* (Survey); the Study Guide Overview (Overview); and the Telelesson Focus Points. Page numbers are also given for the Textbook Focus Points. "KT" indicates questions with Key Terms defined.

Question	Answer	Learning Objective	Textbook Focus Point (page no.)	Telelesson Focus Point
1	A	1	1 (Jones, p. 137; Survey, p. 84)	
2	B	1	1 (Jones, p. 137; Survey, p. 84)	
3	D	1	1 (Jones, p. 137; Survey, p. 84)	
4	A	1	1 (Jones, p. 138; Survey, p. 85)	
5	B	2	2 (Jones, p. 138; Survey, p. 85)	
6	C	2	2 (Jones, p. 140; Survey, p. 86)	
7	B	2	3 (Jones, p. 138; Survey, p. 85)	
8	C	3	4 (Jones, p. 140; Survey, p. 86)	
9	D	4	5 (Jones, pp. 141-142; Survey, pp. 87-88)	
10	D	4	5 (Jones, p. 141)	
11	C	1		1
12	D	2		2
13	A	1		3

Short Answer:

14		3		4

As published by
The New York Times

The Pentagon Papers

The Secret History
of The Vietnam War.

Investigative reporting by Neil Sheehan.
Written by E. W. Kenworthy, Fox Butterfield,

First Amendment Freedoms

Overview

This lesson continues the study of the Bill of Rights, focusing solely on the freedoms guaranteed by the First Amendment to the U.S. Constitution. Another lesson covered individual freedoms, many of which are implied. However, the freedoms covered by the First Amendment are very specific: freedom of religion, freedom of speech, freedom of the press, freedom to assemble peaceably, and freedom to petition the government.

But does this specificity mean that these freedoms are absolute? There are those who believe, as did Justice Hugo Black, that the First Amendment freedoms indeed are absolute, because the amendment clearly states that "Congress shall make no law. . . ." Others support the belief that there are shades of gray, or exceptions, to these freedoms, which people could not have known about when it was adopted.

Yet nearly everyone agrees that a democracy cannot exist without the freedoms spelled out in the First Amendment. Hence, the role of the U.S. Supreme Court in interpreting these freedoms, which we studied earlier, grows in significance and difficulty.

We approach our study of the First Amendment freedoms using the doctrine of "preferred position." This says that these freedoms have the highest priority in our constitutional hierarchy, that they are fundamental if democracy as we know it in the United States is to survive. Many constitutional scholars consider the First Amendment more important than the rest of the Bill of Rights or the other amendments to the Constitution.

We also examine conflicts that have arisen between the First Amendment's absolute guarantees and the exceptions, such as freedom of the press versus our right to a public and fair trial, or freedom to worship as we please versus a threat to our safety. In many cases the Supreme Court has applied the "clear and present danger" test in deciding these issues.

As a result, more restrictions have been placed on the freedom to assemble than on any other First Amendment freedom. But these restrictions have been applied to protect an overriding consideration: the public's safety.

Finally, we look at freedom of expression—the basis for the 1989 Supreme Court decision regarding the right to burn the flag. Our review of the cases involving the Pentagon Papers and *Progressive Magazine* can help us better understand other decisions based on this issue.

The democratic form of government is based on our right to speak freely, to organize into groups, to question the decisions and actions of our government, and, if we want, to campaign openly against these. It is imperative that we understand what our First Amendment rights are, for if we do not know what we have to lose, we may forfeit these precious rights guaranteed by the very First Amendment to our Constitution.

Learning Objectives

Goal: The purpose of "First Amendment Freedoms" is to describe the meaning and judicial interpretation of the freedoms guaranteed by the First Amendment and to assess the impact on these rights of individuals.

Objectives:

1. Explain the two principal precepts of freedom of religion as protected by the First Amendment, focusing on the Supreme Court interpretation of the establishment clause and application of the free exercise clause.

2. List restrictions the Supreme Court has placed on the First Amendment guarantee of freedom of expression, including forms of speech that have been unprotected.

3. Review the applications of, and restrictions placed on, the First Amendment guarantee of freedom of the press, including prior restraint, libel, and censorship.

4. Describe the First Amendment guarantee of freedom to assemble peaceably and to petition the government for a redress of grievances, as well as the limitations placed on these freedoms.

5. Outline the First Amendment freedoms and rights, covering general restrictions, who interprets these freedoms, the importance of citizen awareness, and the effect of *Gitlow v. New York* on court decisions.

6. Describe the "clear and present danger" test as it applies to the First Amendment, especially to freedom of religion and freedom of press.

Key Terms

Watch for these terms and pay particular attention to what each one means, as you follow the textbook and telelesson.

Establishment clause	Slander
Free exercise clause	Libel
Clear and present danger test	"Gag" orders
Preferred-position test	Fairness doctrine
Bad-tendency rule	Preferred position doctrine (TV)
Prior restraint	Wall of separation (TV)
Symbolic speech	"Lemon" test (TV)
Commercial speech	Censorship (TV)
Defamation of character	

Textbook Reading Assignment

Schmidt, Shelley, and Bardes. *American Government and Politics Today*, 1993-94 edition. Chapter 4, "Civil Liberties," pp. 106-124.

Textbook Focus Points

Before you read the textbook assignment, review the following points to help focus your thoughts. After you complete the assignment, write out your responses to reinforce what you have learned.

1. What are the two principal precepts of freedom of religion?

2. How has the Supreme Court interpreted the establishment clause of the First Amendment?

3. How has the free exercise clause of the First Amendment been applied?

4. What restrictions have been placed on the First Amendment freedom of expression?

5. What forms of free speech have been unprotected, and how can you determine if certain speech is protected or not?

6. What restrictions have been placed on the First Amendment freedom of the press?

7. What restrictions have been placed on individuals' freedom to assemble and petition their government, as guaranteed by the First Amendment?

Telelesson Interviewees

The following individuals share their expertise in the telelesson:

Jesse Choper–Dean and Professor of Law, University of California Law School, Berkeley

Kenneth Janda–Professor of Political Science, Northwestern University

Brian Landsberg–Professor, McGeorge School of Law, University of the Pacific

John R. Schmidhauser–Professor of Political Science, University of Southern California, Los Angeles

Telelesson Focus Points

Before viewing the telelesson, read over the following points to help focus your thoughts. After the presentation, write out your responses to help you remember these important points.

1. Who restricts or regulates the First Amendment freedoms, and who determines if these restrictions violate the First Amendment?

2. Why is it important for us to know and understand what our First Amendment rights are?

3. What was the significance of *Gitlow v. New York*, and how has this decision affected subsequent court decisions?

4. What is the clear and present danger test, and how has it been applied to freedom of religion?

5. How has the clear and present danger test been applied to freedom of the press?

6. How has the Supreme Court restricted the freedom of assembly, and how critical is this freedom?

7. Why is it important for us to know what our First Amendment freedoms are?

Recommended Reading

The following suggestions are not required unless your instructor assigns them. They are listed to let you know where you can find additional information on areas which interest you.

Drinan, Robert F. "Do Creches Violate the Constitution?" *America* 159 (November 26, 1988): pp. 428-429.

Faulk, John Henry. *Fear on Trial*. New York: Grosset and Dunlap, 1976.

Karlen, Neal. "Busting the Bhagwan." *Newsweek* 106 (November 11, 1985): pp. 26-32.

Orwell, George. *Nineteen Eighty-Four*. San Diego, California: Harcourt, Brace, Jovanovich; 1983.

Sanders, Alain L. "Revisiting the Reindeer Rule." *Time* 132 (December 12, 1988): p. 71.

"Supreme Court Justice Speaks His Mind on Key Issues." *U.S. News & World Report* 65 (December 16, 1968): pp. 55-57.

"Worldly Guru in the Western World." *U.S. News & World Report* 99 (October 14, 1985): p. 15.

Getting Involved

These activities are not required unless your instructor assigns them. But they offer good suggestions to help you understand and become more involved in the political process.

1. In Oregon, a group of religious adherents, the Rajneeshees, literally took over the town of Antelope. They renamed it Rajneeshpuram, instituted their own concept of a religious state, and frightened away many of the former residents. Write a brief essay on how the freedom to believe and practice religion as you please applies to the rights of the Rajneeshees and to the rights of the earlier inhabitants.

2. Research the Supreme Court decision in *Miller v. California*, which established the criteria for judging obscenity. Do you agree with these standards? What changes would you recommend?

Self Test

After reading the assignment and watching the telelesson, you should be able to answer these questions. When you have completed the test, turn to the Answer Key to score your answers.

1. Freedom of religion consists of two principal precepts, the
    a. acknowledgement of God and the right to pray.
    b. freedom to worship and the right of the government to acknowledge the true faith.
    c. power of the government to regulate religion and the right of religious groups to gain political power.
    d. separation of church and state, and the free exercise of religion.

2. In *Lemon v. Kurtzman*, the court ruled that direct state aid might NOT be used to
    a. provide free lunches to church-related schools.
    b. subsidize religious instruction.
    c. purchase Bibles for religious classes.
    d. fund basic education grants to religious colleges.

3. A person can hold any religious belief, or no belief, but the government can become involved and act when
    a. religion advocates the overthrow of the government.
    b. churches try to avoid paying property taxes.
    c. religious practices harm the public welfare.
    d. churches harbor convicted felons.

4. Which of the following is NOT one of the requirements of the obscenity test established in the 1973 *Miller* ruling?
    a. The work violates contemporary community standards.
    b. The work taken as a whole appeals to prurient interest in sex.
    c. The work provokes a community to demonstrate against it.
    d. The work shows patently offensive sexual conduct.

---

5. Libel is
   a. insurance one must have on a motor vehicle.
   b. defamation in writing.
   c. spoken words that cannot be proven.
   d. printed material that is highly controversial.

6. In regard to the right to assemble, municipalities
   a. have to provide an adequate place for all people to meet.
   b. may require permits for demonstrations.
   c. are prohibited from making any restrictions.
   d. have no power to pass limitations without state approval.

7. Any laws restricting or regulating the First Amendment freedoms have their constitutionality decided by the
   a. Supreme Court.
   b. president.
   c. bureaucracies.
   d. Congress.

8. It is vital to understand what rights are guaranteed by the First Amendment, so that we
   a. will know when they are being infringed upon.
   b. can trust our elected officials to guard them.
   c. can have the president uphold the Constitution.
   d. can be informed if we are called to jury duty.

9. The *Gitlow* v. *New York* decision was the first time the Supreme Court said specifically that First Amendment freedoms
   a. can be restricted in any way by the national government.
   b. apply to state and local governments, as well as to the national government.
   c. are secondary in importance to the laws of state governments.
   d. can be interpreted solely by the U.S. Supreme Court.

10. The test used by the Supreme Court to determine if the liberties guaranteed by the First Amendment can be restricted is known as the
    a. positive law test.
    b. bad-tendency rule.
    c. clear and present danger test.
    d. sliding-scale test.

11. In *Engel v. Vitale*, the Court ruled that any prayer written or sanctioned by state officials to further religious beliefs
    a. is permissible if no specific religion is favored.
    b. teaches school children vital life values.
    c. restricts children's religious creativity.
    d. violates the establishment clause of the First Amendment.

12. The cases of the Pentagon Papers and *Progressive Magazine* centered around the action of "prior restraint," also known as
    a. censorship.
    b. espionage.
    c. a "gag" order.
    d. a restraining order.

13. Because no one has the right to deliberately incite others to violence, block traffic, or hold parades just anywhere at any time, the Supreme Court has decided that the power of local authorities to place reasonable restrictions on large public gatherings is
    a. a violation of people's rights to peaceably assemble.
    b. not an infringement on First Amendment liberties.
    c. an example of the national government's supremacy.
    d. a division of power between national and local governments.

14. It is imperative that we understand what our First Amendment rights are, because the First Amendment is the
    a. only amendment with five provisions.
    b. guarantee to hold free elections.
    c. cornerstone of American democracy.
    d. basis of most lawsuits.

Short-Answer Question:

15. Contrast the "absoluteness" versus the "shades of gray" interpretations of First Amendment freedoms, as they relate to your personal beliefs.

Answer Key

These are the correct answers with reference to the Learning Objectives, and to the source of the information: the Textbook Focus Points, Schmidt, *et al. American Government and Politics Today* (Schmidt), and the Telelesson Focus Points. Page numbers are also given for the Textbook Focus Points. "KT" indicates questions with Key Terms defined.

Question	Answer	Learning Objective	Textbook Focus Point (page no.)	Telelesson Focus Point
1	D	1	1 (Schmidt, p. 106)	
2	B	1	1 (Schmidt, p. 110)	
3	C	1	3 (Schmidt, p. 110)	
4	C	2	4 (Schmidt, p. 114)	
5	B	3	5,6 (Schmidt, p. 119)........KT	
6	B	4	7 (Schmidt, p. 123)	
7	A	5		1
8	A	5		2
9	B	5		3
10	C	6	5 (Schmidt, p. 111)...........KT	4
11	D	6	1,2 (Schmidt, pp. 107-108)KT	4
12	A	6	KT	5
13	B	4		6
14	C	5		7

Short Answer:

15		5		7

Lesson 24

Equal Protection

Overview

In the United States, the constitutional concept of equal rights and equal protection under the law begins with this statement in the Declaration of Independence: "We hold these truths to be self-evident, that all men are created equal, that they are endowed by their Creator with certain unalienable Rights, that among these are Life, Liberty, and the pursuit of Happiness." The Declaration does not speak only of white Anglo-Saxon Protestants or of white, landed Catholics, but of *all* men. If written today, it most certainly would say, "all people."

Equal protection of the law is a constitutional guarantee contained in the Fourteenth Amendment to the Constitution of the United States, which says: "No State shall...deny to any person within its jurisdiction the equal protection of the laws." In simple language, and in concert with other amendments regarding race and gender, this means that states may not discriminate against persons on the basis of their race, national origin, or gender. The Fourteenth Amendment restricts acts of the states, while the Fifth Amendment guarantees equal treatment from the national government.

The equal protection clause of the Fourteenth Amendment has been used to eradicate barriers in schools, public accommodations, jobs, and access to housing. Courts have ruled that separate facilities are inherently unequal. Today public education, from kindergarten through graduate and professional schools, is open to all individuals—without regard to their race, gender, or national origin.

Governments are forbidden to deny employment to individuals because of their race, color, religion, or gender. The Civil Rights Act goes a step further, prohibiting private employers from discriminating because of race, color, national origin, religion, or gender, and amendments and new laws have expanded this idea to outlaw specific discrimination against those with physical handicaps, veterans, and persons over the age of forty.

Under terms of various court decisions, affirmative action programs may set temporary goals, but not quotas. Such programs may give minorities and women certain preferences in initial employment, training, and promotion. But affirmative action is not a protection against firings or layoffs. However, employers may design race-sensitive affirmative action programs, which make up for past acts of discrimination against minorities and women.

Various civil rights acts prohibit discriminating on the basis of race, color, religion, national origin, family status, and gender in the buying, selling, and rental of housing. The major problem with this legislation is that money seldom is provided to administer and enforce these acts.

In Texas, the equal protection clause of the Fourteenth Amendment has been used to expand voting rights by declaring the "white primary" unconstitutional, outlawing the poll tax, and eliminating property as a qualification to vote in local bond elections. Women in Texas have made progress toward equal rights, but legally they often are still treated differently from men. For example, the Texas Court of Criminal Appeals has ruled that exempting from jury duty women "with legal custody of children under ten years of age does not violate . . . equal protection." However, no similar exemption is offered for men.

For more than twenty years, property-poor independent school districts in Texas, those whose property tax base or value is below the state average, have maintained that they were not receiving sufficient money from the state to offer quality education. In the early 1970s, a lawsuit was filed in federal court contending that the way in which Texas funded its public schools violated the equal protection clause of the U.S. Constitution.

This case, *San Antonio v Rodriguez*, was decided by the U.S. Supreme Court. Despite castigating Texas for the manner in which it financed its public schools, calling it unfair and perhaps even discriminatory, the Court found that this did not violate the U.S. Constitution. In fact, the U.S. Supreme Court held that the U.S. Constitution guarantees no "national right" to equal educational opportunity.

Two decades passed before another suit was filed. Since the U.S. Supreme Court had ruled that there was no national right to equal educational opportunity, *Edgewood v Kirby* was filed in a state district court in Texas. The lawsuit alleged that the procedure Texas used to distribute state funds to public schools violated the equal protection clause (Article I, Section 3) and the efficiency clause (Article 7, Section 1) of the *state* constitution. The plaintiffs contended that, under the rights guaranteed by the Texas Constitution, educational opportunity and quality education should not depend on where you live, and that quality education should be available to all children in Texas.

Texas has an intricate system of state and local financing for its public schools. The property tax assessed by local school districts is the primary source of funds for those districts. In 1985-86, the wealthiest district in Texas had $14 million worth of property to tax per student; the poorest district had only $20,000 worth to tax per student.

The inequalities are especially obvious where costs are similar. For example, the Whiteface Independent School District in the Texas panhandle taxed property owners at $0.30 per $100 of property value (meaning that owners of property valued at $100,000 paid just $300 a year in property tax). But the district raised enough to spend $9,646 per student.

The Morton ISD, just north of Whiteface, taxed its property owners at $0.96 per $100 of property value, more than three times as much as its neighboring district. But, while owners of property valued at $100,000 in the Morton I.S.D. paid $960 per year in property tax, that district raised only enough to spend $3,959 per student—less than half the amount spent on each Whiteface I.S.D. child, even though Morton's property owners paid three times more in taxes.

Some school districts have indoor swimming pools, indoor tennis courts; advanced courses in mathematics, chemistry, and physics; and elaborate fine arts programs. Other schools, often in the same county, offer only the basic curriculum; chemistry is offered one year and physics the next—no advanced courses are ever available; fine arts are offered on a limited basis, if at all; and buildings often are in disrepair.

Consequently, in deciding *Edgewood v Kirby*, State District Judge Harley Clark held that "the Texas system of public school financing violates the Texas Constitution." This finding was based on Article 1, Section 3, of the Texas Constitution, which specifies that "all free men . . . have equal rights," and Article 7, Section 1, which requires the "legislature of the state to establish . . . an efficient system of public free schools."

A court of appeals overturned Clark's ruling, but the Texas Supreme Court nullified the appellate court's ruling. The Supreme Court agreed with Judge Clark, holding that the method of financing public education violated the efficiency clause of the state's constitution. *Edgewood v Kirby* illustrates the fact that your rights under the Texas Constitution may be different—and sometimes even more protected—than under the U.S. Constitution.

The predominant theme of this lesson focuses on the consequences of the decision in *Edgewood v Kirby*. When adequate funding is provided to property-poor districts, they should be able to offer improved educational opportunity for their students.

In the telelesson we visit with James Vasquez, superintendent of the Edgewood Independent School District. He describes the effects of poor education on both local communities and the states, and outlines how additional revenues could be used to improve educational opportunities in Edgewood and similar districts.

Karen Potter of the *Fort Worth Star Telegram* explains the meaning of the Texas Supreme Court's decision, while Al Kaufman, the plaintiffs attorney in the *Edgewood* decision, details why a suit was necessary and the legal basis for the suit. Oscar Mauzy, former associate justice of the Supreme Court of Texas, adds another perspective to the court's decision. Finally, Franklin Jones of Texas Southern University relates the decision in *Edgewood v Kirby* to the concept of equal protection.

To make the public schools of Texas more efficient and to provide all students with suitable educational opportunity costs money. It will cost the state money. But, eventually, the increased cost will come from the pockets of taxpayers at both the state and local levels.

However, experts tell us that the better educated our students are, the less likely they are to wind up on welfare rolls. In addition, when 80 percent of the inmates in the Texas prison system are high school dropouts, it is obvious that, if we can reduce the dropout rate, we can reduce the prison population and its attendant costs.

As taxpayers, we can invest our tax dollars to properly educate our young people. Or, we can support them on welfare rolls and in prisons.

Learning Objectives

Goal: The purpose of this lesson is to illustrate the equal protection clause of the U.S. Constitution by reviewing the *Edgewood v Kirby* decision.

Objectives:

1. Explain the equal protection clause of the U.S. Constitution in relation to state and national government, exceptions, and affirmative action.

2. Discuss the need for additional funding of property-poor school districts in Texas, their rationale for suing the state, and the probable outcome of the *Edgewood v Kirby* ruling.

3. Describe the constitutional basis underlying the Texas ruling that methods of funding public education were unconstitutional.

4. Evaluate the need for, and consequences of, equal educational opportunity and the resultant impact of *Edgewood v Kirby* on public education in Texas.

5. Review the social costs of unequal educational opportunity, and suggest how correcting deficiencies will affect society.

Key Terms

Watch for these terms and pay particular attention to what each one means, as you follow the textbook and telelesson.

Equal protection
Affirmative action
Efficiency clause of the Texas Constitution
San Antonio v Rodriguez
Edgewood Independent School District, et al., v Kirby, et al.

Textbook Reading Assignment

There is no textbook reading assignment for this lesson; however, you are responsible for the information contained in the Study Guide "Overview." There will be overview focus points, self-test questions and questions on your unit examination concerning material found in the Study Guide "Overview."

Overview Focus Points

Before you read the assignment, review the following points to help focus your thoughts. After you complete the assignment, write your responses to reinforce what you have learned.

1. What part of the United States Constitution guarantees equal protection on the part of the states? What part of the U.S. Constitution guarantees equal protection from the national government?

2. What are three areas in which the equal protection clause has been used to eradicate barriers based on race, national origin, and gender?

3. What are affirmative action programs designed to do?

4. Why did property-poor districts need additional state funds?

5. What was the constitutional basis of the state district court's decision to hold unconstitutional the method Texas uses to finance its public schools? What was the constitutional basis of the Texas Supreme Court's decision?

6. What will be the ultimate consequence of equal educational opportunity for all students?

Telelesson Interviewees

The following individuals will share their expertise in the telelesson:

Bob Baker–President, Classroom Teachers of Dallas
Franklin Jones–Department of Political Science, Texas Southern University
Al Kaufman–Plaintiffs Attorney, *Edgewood v Kirby*
Oscar Mauzy–Former Associate Justice, Supreme Court of Texas
Karen Potter–Austin Bureau Chief, *Fort Worth Star Telegram*
James Vasquez–Superintendent, Edgewood Independent School District

Telelesson Focus Points

Before viewing the telelesson, read the following points to help focus your thoughts. After the presentation, write your responses to help you remember these important points.

1. Why did property-poor school districts in Texas go to court to challenge the way in which the state distributes state education funds?

2. What does the decision in *Edgewood v Kirby* mean to property-poor school districts?

3. Why is there a need for equal educational opportunity?

4. According to Franklin Jones, what are the social costs of inadequate education? How will correcting educational deficiencies affect these social costs?

5. What is the impact of *Edgewood v Kirby* on Texas, its educational system, and its residents?

Recommended Reading

The following suggestions are not required unless your instructor assigns them. They are listed to let you know where you can find additional information on areas which interest you.

Brauer, Carl. *John F. Kennedy and the Second Reconstruction*. New York: Columbia University Press, 1977.

Brown, George H.; Nan L. Rosen; and Susan T. Hill. *The Condition of Education for Hispanic Americans*. Washington, D.C.: U. S. Government Printing Office, 1980.

Burstgein, Paul. *Discrimination, Jobs, and Politics; The Struggle for Equal Employment Opportunity in the United States since the New Deal*. Chicago: University of Chicago Press, 1985.

Gillespie, Judith, and John Patrick. "Who Gets What in Crystal City," in Forshee, John, *Readings in American Politics and Government*. Washington, D.C.: University Press of America, 1976.

Kozol, Jonathon. *Savage Inequalities: Children in America's Schools*. New York: Harper, 1992.

Morris, Aldon D. *The Origins of the Civil Rights Movement: Black Communities Organizing for Change*. New York: MacMillan, 1985.

Verba, Sidney, and Gary R. Oren. *Equality in America: The View from the Top*. Cambridge, Mass.: Harvard University Press, 1985.

Getting Involved

This activity is not required unless your instructor assigns it. But it offers good suggestions to help you understand and become more involved in the political process.

In the Spring of each year, the Texas Education Agency and local school districts report the results of the TAAS exam. Review results reported by local media. Do students in one area of the state or one area of a city do better than those in other areas? Offer reasons for differences in performance.

Self Test

After reading the assignment and watching the telelesson, you should be able to answer these questions. When you have completed the test, turn to the Answer Key to score your answers.

1. The U.S. Constitution provides that states shall guarantee equal protection to all residents under
   a. Article V.
   b. Article X.
   c. the Fifth Amendment.
   d. the Fourteenth Amendment.

2. Which of the following is NOT protected by the U.S. Constitution's guarantee of equal protection?
   a. Income equality
   b. Public accommodations
   c. Employment
   d. Housing

3. Affirmative action programs are designed to
   a. make up for past acts of discrimination.
   b. set quotas for employment of women and minorities.
   c. discriminate against white males.
   d. eliminate *de jure* segregation.

4. The state district court declared unconstitutional the method Texas used to finance its public school on the basis of the
   a. Fifth and Fourteenth Amendments to the U.S. Constitution.
   b. Fourth and Fourteenth Amendments to the U.S. Constitution.
   c. Fifteenth and One Hundred-fourth Amendments to the Texas Constitution.
   d. equal protection and efficiency clauses of the Texas Constitution.

5. The consequences of *Edgewood v Kirby* should include
   a. lower property taxes for residents of property-poor school districts.
   b. improved educational opportunity for students in property-poor districts.
   c. elimination of a statewide school district and abolition of all independent school districts.
   d. no significant change in educational levels of Texas public school students.

6. Property-poor districts sued the State of Texas because property-poor districts
   a. could not provide an adequate education based on state funds received and local money raised.
   b. no longer received state funds.
   c. were funded by the state with a less generous formula than that of property-wealthy districts.
   d. could not compete successfully with property-wealthy districts in football and basketball.

7. The decision in *Edgewood v Kirby* should mean that property-poor districts can
   a. reduce property taxes.
   b. eliminate user fees.
   c. offer better educational opportunities to their students.
   d. compete successfully in athletics.

8. Texas school districts need to provide equal educational opportunity to insure that each child has the opportunity to
   a. learn to read and write.
   b. succeed in life.
   c. participate in athletics.
   d. be transported by bus to and from school when needed.

9. An increased crime rate, drop-out rate, and number of individuals on welfare are results of
   a. poor economic condition.
   b. poor planning.
   c. inadequate educational systems.
   d. lack of concern on the part of parents of school children.

Short-Answer Questions:
10. Explain the rationale underlying the lawsuit filed by property-poor school districts against the state of Texas.

11. Describe three probable results of equalized funding for public education among property-poor districts and property-rich districts.

Answer Key

These are the correct answers with reference to the Learning Objectives, and to the source of the information: the Textbook Focus Points, Jones, *et al. Practicing Texas Politics* (Jones) or Jones, *et. al.,* *Practicing Texas Politics — A Brief Survey* (Survey); the Study Guide Overview (Overview); and the Telelesson Focus Points. Page numbers are also given for the Textbook Focus Points. "KT" indicates questions with Key Terms defined.

Question	Answer	Learning Objective	Textbook Focus Point (page no.)	Telelesson Focus Point
1	D	1	1 (Overview)	KT
2	A	1	2 (Overview)	
3	A	1	3 (Overview)	KT
4	D	3	5 (Overview)	
5	B	4	4 (Overview)	
6	A	2		1
7	C	2		2
8	B	4		4
9	C	5		4

Short Answers:

10		2		1
11		4		5

Lesson 25

Women and Minorities

Overview

This lesson completes our study of *Government by Consent*, bringing together concepts and institutional structures we have studied throughout the course. Elsewhere we saw how the Fourteenth Amendment has been used to apply the Bill of Rights to the states through selective incorporation. The "equal protection of the laws" clause of that amendment also serves as the basis for many of the cases filed by women and minority groups. In this lesson, we see how these groups apply this clause in arguing their cases.

Minority groups, especially blacks or African-Americans, have been very successful with the courts; probably the best known and most widely beneficial case is the 1954 decision in Brown v. Board of Education. These groups also have succeeded in having legislation passed to establish and protect their rights as full citizens, such as the 1964 Civil Rights Act, the Voting Rights Act, and the Equal Pay Act.

So far women, however, have not enjoyed the same results, even though they are a majority of the electorate. During the Civil War period many activist women made a conscious decision to push for rights for blacks first, since African-Americans then certainly were in worse straits than women. But it took fifty more years —from 1870 when black men were fully enfranchised, until 1920—for women to simply gain the right to vote. (If you have a grandmother or great-grandmother over age 70 in 1990, she was born without the right to vote if she grew up as a citizen in the United States.)

Working to get the Equal Rights Amendment passed by Congress and presented to the states for ratification took yet another fifty years. Then it was ratified by the majority of state legislatures, but it failed to achieve approval by the required three-fourths of the states and died. This lesson briefly covers what the ERA wanted to achieve, why it failed, and the various ways the ERA and less permanent guarantees of equality for women are being re-introduced in Congress.

The term "equality" often is used synonymously with civil rights: the personal freedoms guaranteed in this country by the Constitution, its amendments, and the laws enacted by Congress. Yet the action toward equality has moved from primarily equal treatment regardless of race, to more equal treatment or equal opportunity for all in the economic and political arenas. This does not overlook the fact that the struggle for racial equality continues; simply that it does so to a lesser degree than the struggle for economic and political equality.

In this lesson we not only examine how and why the civil rights movement in the United States evolved for minority groups and for women, we also assess the current status of civil rights for all. At the same time we examine some of the new problems raised by attempts to solve equality issues.

In short, the struggle for civil rights seems to be perpetual, with only specific issues resolved, one at a time. Equality issues today are broader and more complex than the comparatively simple issue of racial equality; current issues include such concerns as affirmative action, comparable worth, abortion decisions, reverse discrimination, and gay rights. These issues not only involve "balancing acts" similar to those we encounter in criminal justice— trying to be equally fair to both sides—they often come to the forefront based on the so-called "pocketbook issues."

Both minorities and women have come a long way in their fight for equality under the law of the United States of America. The struggle has been neither easy nor static, for the issues and their context change over time. Perhaps the words of Martin Luther King Jr. best sum up the reason why the struggle for legal equality for everyone —with constitutional guarantees—continues: "Injustice anywhere is a threat to justice everywhere."

Learning Objectives

Goal: The purpose of "Women and Minorities" is to describe how women and minorities historically have not enjoyed the same treatment under the law as white males, and to explain how the Fourteenth Amendment, legislation, and judicial interpretation are used to advance the civil rights of all.

Objectives:

1. Describe the types of discrimination against blacks, beginning with their status prior to the Civil War through the nonviolent activities of the 1960s civil rights movement, and how the civil rights legislation it produced has affected American society since then.

2. Explain in what ways the difficulty that Hispanics (Latinos) have had, in entering the political mainstream and achieving power, differ from the problems faced by African-Americans.

3. Describe how the legal status of the American Indian differs from that of other minorities and women, as well as what the U.S. government has done to address the unique problems of these Native Americans.

4. Contrast the types of discrimination toward Asian-Americans in the past with that experienced today.

5. Outline the struggle for equality for all people, including the revised concept of the "melting pot" and projections of new issues in civil rights.

6. Highlight the various forms of discrimination against women, beginning with women's struggle to gain suffrage and continuing through current efforts to make them equal citizens in every respect, then highlight the effects of legislation and judicial decisions on their progress.

7. List the major problems facing the elderly today, along with what attempts are being made to alleviate these problems.

8. Review actions taken to increase public awareness and protect the rights of handicapped individuals, as well as how such action benefits the rest of society.

9. Describe the rights of juveniles, considering the low status in which they are seemingly held.

10. Outline the rights of the gay population and the roles organized groups are playing in American politics.

11. Analyze the impact of the black civil rights movement on other groups that were not, or still may not be, receiving equal treatment under the law.

Key Terms

Watch for these terms and pay particular attention to what each one means, as you follow the textbook and telelesson.

"Separate but equal" doctrine
De facto segregation
De jure segregation
Busing
Equal Employment Opportunity
  Commission
Affirmative action

Reverse discrimination
White primary
Poll tax
Suffrage
Sex discrimination
Sexual harassment
Comparable worth

Textbook Reading Assignment

Schmidt, Shelley, and Bardes. *American Government and Politics Today*, 1993-94 edition. Chapter 5, "Minority Rights," pp. 139-176, and Chapter 6, "Striving for Equality," pp.177-206.

Textbook Focus Points

Before you read the textbook assignment, review the following points to help focus your thoughts. After you complete the assignment, write out your responses to reinforce what you have learned.

1. Outline the legal status of blacks prior to the Civil War, and from then until the 1960s civil rights movement.

2. Describe the nonviolent activities of the 1960s civil rights movement.

3. Explain the major civil rights legislation of the 1960s and its effect on American society.

4. If the Fifteenth Amendment gave everyone, except women, the right to vote, why was the Voting Rights Act of 1965 necessary, and what did the act provide?

5. Why have Hispanics had difficulty achieving political power, and what attempts have they made to enter the political mainstream?

6. How do Native Americans differ from other minorities and women in legal terms, and what has the government done to address this situation?

7. How and why have Asian-Americans experienced discrimination at various times in U.S. history, including today?

8. How is the "melting pot" idea being revised now?

9. Describe the struggle of women in the United States to gain "suffrage," the right to vote.

10. What are some of the major arenas in which women are still struggling to achieve equal status?

11. How has the federal government responded to different types of sex discrimination in jobs?

12. What are the major problems of elderly people today, and what are they doing to try to alleviate these problems?

13. What actions have handicapped individuals taken to bring their needs to the public's attention, and what actions has the government taken to protect their rights?

14. What rights do juveniles have, and why is their status so low?

15. What rights do gays have, and what role are they playing in American politics?

Telelesson Interviewees

The following individuals share their expertise in the telelesson:

Richard L. Dockery–Member of the Clergy; Southwest Regional Director, National Association for the Advancement of Colored People

Andy Hernandez–President, Southwest Voter Registration Education Project

Eleanor Holmes Norton–Professor, Georgetown University Law School

Barbara Jordan–Attorney and Professor, LBJ School of Public Affairs, University of Texas, Austin

Randall Kennedy–Professor, Harvard University Law School

Sarah Weddington–Attorney; Associate Professor of Government and American Studies, University of Texas, Austin

Telelesson Focus Points

Before viewing the telelesson, read over the following points to help focus your thoughts. After the presentation, write out your responses to help you remember these important points.

1. Why is the struggle for equality so difficult?

2. How did the black civil rights movement affect later efforts by other minority groups?

3. How have blacks struggled to gain their civil rights, and what are some of the remedies prescribed to resolve this situation?

4. How were women "protected" by laws, even after they were guaranteed the right to vote?

5. What have women done to raise themselves above "second class" status?

6. Why has it been difficult for Hispanics to gain civil rights?

7. According to Randall Kennedy, what new civil rights issues will we be facing?

Recommended Reading

The following suggestions are not required unless your instructor assigns them. They are listed to let you know where you can find additional information on areas which interest you.

Blow, Richard. "Those Were the Gays." *New Republic* 197 (November 2, 1987): pp. 14-16+.

Brown, Dee. *Bury My Heart at Wounded Knee.* New York: Holt, Rinehart and Winston, 1971.

Davidson, Bill. "Our Largest Minority: Americans with Handicaps." *McCalls* 114 (September 1987): pp. 61-68.

Friedan, Betty. *The Feminine Mystique.* New York: W.W. Norton, 1963.

Gibbs, Nancy R. "Grays on the Go." *Time* 131 (February 22, 1988): pp. 66-70+.

Griffin, John H. *Black Like Me.* Boston: Houghton Mifflin Co., 1977.

King, Martin Luther, Jr. "Letter from the Birmingham Jail." In *A Testament of Hope,* edited by James Melvin Washington. San Francisco: Harper & Row, 1986. [Reprinted with permission at the end of this Study Guide.]

Mansbridge, Jane J. *Why We Lost the E.R.A.* Chicago: University of Chicago Press, 1986.

McCormick, John. "America's Third World." *Newsweek* 112 (August 8, 1988): pp. 20-24+.

Meyer, Dylan S. *Uprooted American: The Japanese-American and the War Relocation Authority During World War II.* Tucson: University of Arizona Press, 1971.

Ramirez, Anthony. "America's Super Minority." *Fortune* 114 (November 24, 1986): pp. 148-149+.

Whitman, David. "For Latinos, A Growing Divide." *U.S. News & World Report* 103 (August 10, 1987): pp. 47-49.

Getting Involved

These activities are not required unless your instructor assigns them. But they offer good suggestions to help you understand and become more involved in the political process.

1. Note the "Getting Involved" sections in your textbook at the end of Chapters 5 and 6.

2. Participate in a Handicapped Awareness Week, so that you can become more aware of the problems that a handicapped person frequently encounters and the need for additional legislative protection.

Self Test

After reading the assignment and watching the telelesson, you should be able to answer these questions. When you have completed the test, turn to the Answer Key to score your answers.

1. Prior to any amendments to the United States Constitution, slaves were
   a. illegal because of the language of Article I.
   b. to be freed after twenty-five years except in the southern states.
   c. referred to as "other persons."
   d. essential for a free-market economy.

2. The Supreme Court invalidated the 1875 Civil Rights Act because the Fourteenth Amendment was
   a. held to be unconstitutional.
   b. depriving minorities of their basic rights.
   c. an attempt to end discrimination by allowing reverse discrimination.
   d. aimed at limiting state action, not actions of private citizens.

3. In the case of *Brown v. Board of Education* (1954), the Supreme Court held that
   a. ethnic minorities have no right to equal treatment by the government.
   b. public-school segregation of races violates the equal protection clause of the Fourteenth Amendment.
   c. the national government does not have the power to force any type of action on local school boards.
   d. the separation of races for a reason like education is not a violation of the Constitution.

4. The civil rights movement led by Martin Luther King Jr. was based on the philosophy of
   a. nonviolent civil disobedience.
   b. divide and conquer.
   c. "equality for all, through strong force when necessary."
   d. equality of practice that did not have to exclude racial segregation.

5. The Civil Rights Acts of 1964 and 1968 and the Voting Rights Act of 1965 marked the resumption by Congress of a leading role in
   a. deciding domestic policies rather than leaving them to the president.
   b. becoming involved in interstate commerce as it affects the national trade policy.
   c. enforcing the constitutional idea of equality for all Americans.
   d. lawmaking, rather than reacting to the proposals of the president and bureaucratic agencies.

6. Title VII of the Civil Rights Act of 1964 forms the cornerstone of employment-discrimination law, because it prohibits discrimination in employment based on
   a. abusive child-labor laws.
   b. race, color, religion, sex, or national origin.
   c. description and responsibilities of the job.
   d. membership in labor unions.

7. One of the major provisions of the Voting Rights Act of 1965 was to
   a. eliminate discriminatory voter-registration tests.
   b. give members of all races the opportunity to vote.
   c. let state governments make all decisions about voting requirements.
   d. end the preponderance of males holding public office.

8. Even though Hispanics represent over 8 percent of the American population, they have had difficulty achieving political power, particularly at the national level, because they have
   a. few strong leaders and low voter turnout.
   b. placed little emphasis on education.
   c. problems finding employment and speaking English.
   d. great national diversity and geographical dispersion.

9. A major distinction between American Indians and other ethnic minorities is that Native Americans were
   a. never discriminated against.
   b. designated by Congress to be citizens of foreign nations.
   c. not given rights that are protected by the Constitution.
   d. not qualified to become citizens for religious reasons.

10. Asian Americans typically are not thought of as being discriminated against because they
   a. are a very new group in the United States.
   b. have considerable representation in Congress.
   c. do not attempt to resist racial discrimination.
   d. earn a relatively high median income.

11. The revision of the "melting pot" idea is happening due to a new emphasis on
   a. excluding groups that are not willing to accept traditional American values.
   b. legislation that would restrict the number of immigrants to the United States.
   c. majority rights as opposed to minority rights.
   d. ethnic and racial pride.

12. The first political cause in which women as a group became active was the
   a. abolition movement.
   b. right to vote.
   c. right to own property without masculine approval.
   d. equal rights movement.

13. The representation of women in political office
    a. is considerably less today than it was in the first years after the Nineteenth Amendment.
    b. exceeds the percentage of voters who are women.
    c. is higher in the United States than in any other country.
    d. does not reflect the participation of women as voters.

14. The prospects for ratification of an Equal Rights Amendment may be
    a. uncertain, but the National Organization for Women and related groups, however, continue the struggle.
    b. slim, because a majority of Americans are opposed to such action.
    c. finished for this century, because a rejected amendment cannot be re-submitted for fifty years.
    d. very poor, because most women now think that such an amendment would greatly hurt their social position.

15. With reference to women's rights, protective legislation is legislation
    a. that prohibits women from becoming military officers.
    b. that protects a woman's inheritance from her husband.
    c. that seeks to protect the health and morals of women.
    d. that prohibits women from taking jobs deemed too dangerous or strenuous.

16. A major change in society's attitude toward age today stems from the growing number of
    a. births, compared to the "baby boom" era.
    b. people age 65 or over.
    c. teenagers.
    d. elderly not reaching their predicted life expectancy.

17. Congress passed the Rehabilitation Act in 1973, which prohibited discrimination against people with a handicap
    a. by prohibiting any reference to a handicap on job applications.
    b. by providing job training and placement programs.
    c. in programs receiving federal aid.
    d. in areas of employment where a handicap was not a factor.

18. The largest group of individuals in the United States with the smallest amount of rights and protection are
    a. women.
    b. Mexican-Americans.
    c. the elderly.
    d. children.

19. The rights and status of homosexuals was ruled upon by the Supreme Court in a case from the state of Georgia in 1986, in which the court held that
    a. state governments cannot discriminate against "gay" sexual conduct.
    b. engaging in homosexual sodomy is not a fundamental right.
    c. people have a fundamental right to practice sexual conduct without government interference.
    d. sexual conduct is a state concern over which the Supreme Court has no jurisdiction.

20. In one sense, the battle for full equality can never be over because
    a. equality is an ideal that can never be achieved.
    b. minority groups do not know how to achieve full equality.
    c. the goals of many minorities change as they progress up the equality ladder.
    d. minorities are never satisfied with their achievements.

21. The black civil rights movement paved the way for later efforts by other minority groups by
    a. using legislation instead of the courts.
    b. using violence as a method of demonstration.
    c. giving them hope that they too might succeed.
    d. dividing minorities in establishing a common goal.

22. In 1896 in *Plessy v. Ferguson*, the Supreme Court ruled that blacks could not be denied equality, but said the
    a. threat of a clear and present danger existed.
    b. no pain/no gain doctrine was applicable.
    c. heterogeneous segregation doctrine was exemplified.
    d. separate and equal concept was acceptable.

23. Which of the following was NOT used as a basis for denying women their civil rights in order to "protect" them?
    a. Running for political office would expose them to vulgarity and sinful vices.
    b. The paternalistic system labeled them weaker and more fragile than men.
    c. Politics would destroy their femininity and harden their personal values.
    d. They would have to meet the same requirements as their male counterparts.

24. Which of the following ways is the only one that does NOT show that women were gaining political power during the 1972 presidential campaign?
    a. A woman was named chair of a national party.
    b. A record number of women were convention delegates.
    c. More women than men voted.
    d. Political campaigns were staffed primarily by women volunteers.

25. Hispanics, the second-largest ethnic minority group in the United States, often face the additional challenge of
    a. a question of identity.
    b. a void of leadership.
    c. a language barrier.
    d. an economic drought.

26. Randall Kennedy states that, in the past, we have thought of the race question as a black/white issue, but the race issue of the future will be part of the larger issue of
    a. politics.
    b. difference.
    c. age.
    d. economics.

Short-Answer Questions:

27. Do you believe that American society has become a "melting pot" or an "ethnic stew"? Why?

28. In terms of discrimination, explain Martin Luther King Jr.'s statement: "Injustice anywhere is a threat to justice everywhere."

Answer Key

These are the correct answers with reference to the Learning Objectives, and to the source of the information: the Textbook Focus Points, Schmidt, *et al. American Government and Politics Today* (Schmidt), and the Telelesson Focus Points. Page numbers are also given for the Textbook Focus Points. "KT" indicates questions with Key Terms defined.

Question	Answer	Learning Objective	Textbook Focus Point (page no.)	Telelesson Focus Point
1	C	1	1 (Schmidt, p. 142)	
2	D	1	1 (Schmidt, p. 144)	
3	B	1	1 (Schmidt, p. 145)	
4	A	1	2 (Schmidt, p. 149)	
5	C	1	3 (Schmidt, p. 153)	
6	B	1	3 (Schmidt, p. 154)	
7	A	1	4 (Schmidt, p. 159)	
8	D	2	5 (Schmidt, p. 161)	
9	B	3	6 (Schmidt, p. 166)	
10	D	4	7 (Schmidt, p. 168)	
11	D	5	8 (Schmidt, p. 170)	
12	A	6	9 (Schmidt, p. 179)	
13	D	6	10 (Schmidt, p. 181)	
14	A	6	10 (Schmidt, p. 185)	
15	D	6	11 (Schmidt, p. 185)	
16	B	7	12 (Schmidt, p. 191)	
17	C	8	13 (Schmidt, p. 195)	
18	D	9	14 (Schmidt, p. 198)	
19	B	10	15 (Schmidt, p. 202)	
20	A	5		1
21	C	11		2
22	D	1	KT	3
23	D	6		4
24	A	6		5
25	C	2		6
26	B	5		7

Short Answer:

27		5	8 (Schmidt, p. 169-171)	
28		11		1

Letter From Birmingham City Jail

by Martin Luther King, Jr.

Dr. King wrote this famous essay (written in the form of an open letter) on 16 April 1963 while in jail. He was serving a sentence for participating in civil rights demonstrations in Birmingham, Alabama. He rarely took time to defend himself against his opponents. But eight prominent "liberal" Alabama clergymen, all white, published an open letter earlier in January that called on King to allow the battle for integration to continue in the local and federal courts, and warned that King's nonviolent resistance would have the effect of inciting civil disturbances. Dr. King wanted Christian ministers to see that the meaning of Christian discipleship was at the heart of the African American struggle for freedom, justice, and equality.

My Dear Fellow Clergymen,

While confined here in the Birmingham city jail, I came across your recent statement calling our present activities "unwise and untimely." Seldom, if ever, do I pause to answer criticism of my work and ideas. If I sought to answer all of the criticisms that cross my desk, my secretaries would be engaged in little else in the course of the day, and I would have no time for constructive work. But since I feel that you are men of genuine good will and your criticisms are sincerely set forth, I would like to answer your statement in what I hope will be patient and reasonable terms.

I think I should give the reason for my being in Birmingham, since you have been influenced by the argument of "outsiders coming in." I have the honor of serving as president of the Southern Christian Leadership Conference, an organization operating in every southern state, with headquarters in Atlanta, Georgia. We have some eighty-five affiliate organizations all across the South—one being the Alabama Christian Movement for Human Rights. Whenever necessary and possible we share staff, educational and financial resources with our affiliates. Several months ago our local affiliate here in Birmingham invited us to be on call to engage in a nonviolent direct-action program if such were deemed necessary. We readily consented and when the hour came we lived up to our promises. So I am here, along with several members of my staff, because we were invited here. I am here because I have basic organizational ties here.

Beyond this, I am in Birmingham because injustice is here. Just as the eighth century prophets left their little villages and carried their "thus sayith the Lord" far beyond the boundaries of their hometowns; and just as the Apostle Paul left his little Tarsus and carried the gospel of Jesus Christ to practically every hamlet and city of the Graeco-Roman world, I too am compelled to carry the gospel of reedom beyond

---

my particular hometown. Like Paul, I must constantly respond to the Macedonian call for aid.

Moreover, I am cognizant of the interrelatedness of all communities and states. I cannot sit idly by in Atlanta and not be concerned about what happens in Birmingham. Injustice anywhere is a threat to justice everywhere. We are caught in an inescapable network of mutuality, tied in a single garment of destiny. Whatever affects one directly affects all indirectly. Never again can we afford to live with the narrow, provincial "outside agitator" idea. Anyone who lives in the United States can never be considered an outsider anywhere in this country.

You deplore the demonstrations that are presently taking place in Birmingham. But I am sorry that your statement did not express a similar concern for the conditions that brought the demonstrations into being. I am sure that each of you would want to go beyond the superficial social analyst who looks merely at effects, and does not grapple with underlying causes. I would not hesitate to say that it is unfortunate that so-called demonstrations are taking place in Birmingham at this time, but I would say in more emphatic terms that it is even more unfortunate that the white power structure of this city left the Negro community with no other alternative.

In any nonviolent campaign there are four basic steps: (1) collection of the facts to determine whether injustices are alive, (2) negotiation, (3) self-purification, and (4) direct action. We have gone through all of these steps in Birmingham. There can be no gainsaying of the fact that racial injustice engulfs this community.

Birmingham is probably the most thoroughly segregated city in the United States. Its ugly record of police brutality is known in every section of this country. Its injust treatment of Negroes in the courts is a notorious reality. There have been more unsolved bombings of Negro homes and churches in Birmingham than any city in this nation. These are the hard, brutal and unbelievable facts. On the basis of these conditions Negro leaders sought to negotiate with the city fathers. But the political leaders consistently refused to engage in good faith negotiation.

Then came the opportunity last September to talk with some of the leaders of the economic community. In these negotiating sessions certain promises were made by the merchants—such as the promise to remove the humiliating racial signs from the stores. On the basis of these promises Rev. Shuttlesworth and the leaders of the Alabama Christian Movement for Human Rights agreed to call a moratorium on any type of demonstrations. As the weeks and months unfolded we realized that we were the victims of a broken promise. The signs remained. Like so many experiences of the past we were confronted with blasted hopes, and the dark shadow of a deep disappointment settled upon us. So we had no alternative except that of preparing for direct action, whereby we would present our very bodies as a means of laying our case before the conscience of the local and national community. We were not unmindful of the difficulties involved. So we decided to go through a process of self-purification. We started having workshops on nonviolence and repeatedly asked ourselves the questions, "Are you able to accept blows without retaliating?" "Are you able to endure the ordeals of jail?" We decided to set our direct-action program around the Easter season, realizing that with the exception of Christmas, this was the largest shopping period of the year. Knowing that a strong economic withdrawal program would be the by-product of direct action, we felt that this was the best time to bring pressure on the merchants for the needed changes. Then it occurred to us that the March election was ahead and so we speedily decided to postpone action until after election day. When we discovered that Mr. Connor was in the run-off, we decided again to postpone action so that the demonstrations could not be used to cloud the issues. At this time we agreed to begin our nonviolent witness the day after the run-off.

This reveals that we did not move irresponsibly into direct action. We too wanted to see Mr. Connor defeated; so we went through postponement after postponement to aid in this community need. After this we felt that direct action could be delayed no longer.

You may well ask, "Why direct action? Why sit-ins, marches, etc.? Isn't negotiation a better path?" You are exactly right in your call for negotiation. Indeed, this is the purpose of direct action. Nonviolent direct action seeks to create such a crisis and establish such creative tension that a community that has constantly refused to negotiate is forced to confront the issue. It seeks so to dramatize the issue that it can no longer be ignored. I just referred to the creation of tension as a part of the work of the nonviolent resister. This may sound rather shocking. But I must confess that I am not afraid of the word tension. I have earnestly worked and preached against violent tension, but there is a type of constructive nonviolent tension that is necessary for growth. Just as Socrates felt that it was necessary to create a tension in the mind so that individuals could rise from the bondage of myths and half-truths to the unfettered realm of creative analysis and objective appraisal, we must see the need of having nonviolent gadflies to create the kind of tension in society that will help men to rise from the dark depths of prejudice and racism to the majestic heights of understanding and brotherhood. So the purpose of the direct action is to create a situation so crisis-packed that it will inevitably open the door to negotiation. We, therefore, concur with you in your call for negotiation. Too long has our beloved Southland been bogged down in the tragic attempt to live in monologue rather than dialogue.

One of the basic points in your statement is that our acts are untimely. Some have asked, "Why didn't you give the new administration time to act?" The only answer that I can give to this inquiry is that the new administration must be prodded about as much as the outgoing one before it acts. We will be sadly mistaken if we feel that the election of Mr. Boutwell will bring the millennium to Birmingham. While Mr. Boutwell is much more articulate and gentle than Mr. Connor, they are both segregationists, dedicated to the task of maintaining the status quo. The hope I see in Mr. Boutwell is that he will be reasonable enough to see the futility of massive resistance to desegregation. But he will not see this without pressure from the devotees of civil rights. My friends, I must say to you that we have not made a single gain in civil rights without determined legal and nonviolent pressure. History is the long and tragic story of the fact that privileged groups seldom give up their privileges voluntarily. Individuals may see the moral light and voluntarily give up their unjust posture; but as Reinhold Niebuhr has reminded us, groups are more immoral than individuals.

We know through painful experience that freedom is never voluntarily given by the oppressor; it must be demanded by the oppressed. Frankly, I have never yet engaged in a direct action movement that was "well-timed," according to the timetable of those who have not suffered unduly from the disease of segregation. For years now I have heard the words "Wait!" It rings in the ear of every Negro with a piercing familiarity. This "Wait" has almost always meant "Never." It has been a tranquilizing thalidomide, relieving the emotional stress for a moment, only to give birth to an ill-formed infant of frustration. We must come to see with the distinguished jurist of yesterday that "justice too long delayed is justice denied." We have waited for more than 340 years for our constitutional and God-given rights. The nations of Asia and Africa are moving with jetlike speed toward the goal of political independence, and we still creep at horse and buggy pace toward the gaining of a cup of coffee at a lunch counter. I guess it is easy for those who have never felt the stinging darts of segregation to say, "Wait." But when you have seen vicious mobs lynch your mothers and fathers at will and drown your sisters and brothers at whim; when you have seen hate-filled policemen curse, kick, brutalize and even kill your black brothers and sisters with impunity; when you see the vast majority of your twenty million Negro brothers smothering in an airtight cage of poverty in the midst of an affluent society; when you suddenly find your tongue twisted and your speech stammering as you seek to explain to your six-year-old daughter why she can't go to the public amusement park that has just been advertised on television, and see tears welling up in her little eyes when she is told that Funtown is closed to colored children, and see the depressing clouds of inferiority begin to form in her little mental sky, and see her begin to distort her little personality by unconsciously developing a bitterness toward white people; when you have to concoct an answer for a five-year-old son asking in agonizing pathos: "Daddy, why do white people treat colored people so mean?"; when you take a cross-country drive and find it necessary to sleep night after night in the uncomfortable corners of your automobile because no motel will accept you; when you are humiliated day in and day out by nagging signs reading "white" and "colored"; when your first name becomes "nigger" and your middle name becomes "boy" (however old you are) and your last name becomes "John," and when your wife and mother are never given the respected title "Mrs."; when you are harried by day and haunted by night by the fact that you are a Negro, living constantly at tiptoe stance never quite knowing what to expect next, and plagued with inner fears and outer resentments; when you are forever fighting a degenerating sense of "nobodiness"; then you will understand why we find it difficult to wait. There comes a time when the cup of endurance runs over, and men are no longer willing to be plunged into an abyss of injustice where they experience the blackness of corroding despair. I hope, sirs, you can understand our legitimate and unavoidable impatience.

You express a great deal of anxiety over our willingness to break laws. This is certainly a legitimate concern. Since we so diligently urge people to obey the Supreme Court's decision of 1954 outlawing segregation in the public schools, it is rather strange and paradoxical to find us consciously breaking laws. One may well ask, "How can you advocate breaking some laws and obeying others?" The answer is found in the fact that there are two types of laws: there are *just* and there are *unjust* laws. I would agree with Saint Augustine that "An unjust law is no law at all." Now what is the difference between the two? How does one determine when a law is just or unjust? A just law is a man-made code that squares with the moral law or the law of God. An unjust law is a code that is out of harmony with the moral law. To put it in the terms of Saint Thomas Aquinas, an unjust law is a human law that is not rooted in eternal and natural law. Any law that uplifts human personality is just. Any law that degrades human personality is unjust. All segregation statutes are unjust because segregation distorts the soul and damages the personality. It gives the segregator a false sense of superiority, and the segregated a false sense of inferiority. To use the words of Martin Buber, the great Jewish philosopher, segregation substitutes an "I-it" relationship for the "I-thou" relationship, and ends up relegating persons to the status of things. So segregation is not only politically, economically and sociologically unsound, but it is morally wrong and sinful. Paul Tillich has said that sin is separation. Isn't segregation an existential expression of man's tragic separation, an expression of his awful estrangement, his terrible sinfulness? So I can urge men to disobey segregation ordinances because they are morally wrong.

Let us turn to a more concrete example of just and unjust laws. An unjust law is a code that a majority inflicts on a minority that is not binding on itself. This is difference made legal. On the other hand a just law is a code that a majority compels a minority to follow that it is willing to follow itself. This is sameness made legal.

Let me give another explanation. An unjust law is a code inflicted upon a minority which that minority had no part in enacting or creating because they did not have the unhampered right to vote. Who can say that the legislature of Alabama which set up the segregation laws was democratically elected? Throughout the state of Alabama all types of conniving methods are used to prevent Negroes from becoming registered voters and there are some counties without a single Negro registered to vote despite the fact that the Negro constitutes a majority of the population. Can any law set up in such a state be considered democratically structured?

These are just a few examples of unjust and just laws. There are some instances when a law is just on its face and unjust in its application. For instance, I was arrested Friday on a charge of parading without a permit. Now there is nothing wrong with an ordinance which requires a permit for a parade, but when the ordinance is used to preserve segregation and to deny citizens the First Amendment privilege of peaceful assembly and peaceful protest, then it becomes unjust.

I hope you can see the distinction I am trying to point out. In no sense do I advocate evading or defying the law as the rabid segregationist would do. This would lead to anarchy. One who breaks an unjust law must do it *openly, lovingly* (not hatefully as the white mothers did in New Orleans when they were seen on television screaming, "nigger, nigger, nigger"), and with a willingness to accept the penalty. I submit that an individual who breaks a law that conscience tells him is unjust, and willingly accepts the penalty by staying in jail to arouse the conscience of the community over its injustice, is in reality expressing the very highest respect for the law.

Of course, there is nothing new about this kind of civil disobedience. It was seen sublimely in the refusal of Shadrach, Meshach, and Abednego to obey the laws of Nebuchadnezzar because a higher moral law was involved. It was practiced superbly by the early Christians who were willing to face hungry lions and the excruciating pain of chopping blocks, before submitting to certain unjust laws of the Roman Empire. To a degree academic freedom is a reality today because Socrates practiced civil disobedience.

We can never forget that everything Hitler did in Germany was "legal" and everything the Hungarian freedom fighters did in Hungary was "illegal." It was "illegal" to aid and comfort a Jew in Hitler's Germany. But I am sure that if I had lived in Germany during that time I would have aided and comforted my Jewish brothers even though it was illegal. If I lived in a Communist country today where certain principles dear to the Christian faith are suppressed, I believe I would openly advocate disobeying these anti-religious laws. I must make two honest confessions to you, my Christian and Jewish brothers. First, I must confess that over the last few years I have been gravely disappointed with the white moderate. I have almost reached the regrettable conclusion that the Negro's great stumbling block in the stride toward freedom is not the White Citizen's Counciler or the Ku Klux Klanner, but the white moderate who is more devoted to "order" than to justice; who prefers a negative peace which is the absence of tension to a positive peace which is the presence of justice; who constantly says, "I agree with you in the goal you seek, but I can't agree with your methods of direct action"; who paternalistically feels that he can set the timetable for another man's freedom; who lives by the myth of time and who constantly advised the Negro to wait until a "more convenient season." Shallow understanding from people of good will is more frustrating than absolute misunderstanding from people of ill will. Lukewarm acceptance is much more bewildering than outright rejection.

I had hoped that the white moderate would understand that law and order exist for the purpose of establishing justice, and that when they fail to do this they become dangerously structured dams that block the flow of social progress. I had hoped that the white moderate would understand that the present tension of the South is merely a necessary phase of the transition from an obnoxious negative peace, where the Negro passively accepted his unjust plight, to a substance-filled positive peace, where all men will respect the dignity and worth of human personality. Actually, we who engage in nonviolent direct action are not the creators of tension. We merely bring to the surface the hidden tension that is already alive. We bring it out in the open where it can be seen and dealt with. Like a boil that can never be cured as long as it is covered up but must be opened with all its pus-flowing ugliness to the natural medicines of air and light, injustice must likewise be exposed, with all of the tension its exposing creates, to the light of human conscience and the air of national opinion before it can be cured.

In your statement you asserted that our actions, even though peaceful, must be condemned because they precipitate violence. But can this assertion be logically made? Isn't this like condemning the robbed man because his possession of money precipitated the evil act of robbery? Isn't this like condemning Socrates because his unswerving commitment to truth and his philosophical delvings precipitated the misguided popular mind to make him drink the hemlock? Isn't this like condemning Jesus because His unique God-consciousness and never-ceasing devotion to his will precipitated the evil act of crucifixion? We must come to see, as federal courts have consistently affirmed, that it is immoral to urge an individual to withdraw his efforts to gain his basic constitutional rights because the quest precipitates violence. Society must protect the robbed and punish the robber.

I had also hoped that the white moderate would reject the myth of time. I received a letter this morning from a white brother in Texas which said: "All Christians know that the colored people will receive equal rights eventually, but it is possible that you are in too great of a religious hurry. It has taken Christianity almost two thousand years to accomplish what it has. The teachings of Christ take time to come to earth." All that is said here grows out of a tragic misconception of time. It is the strangely irrational notion that there is something in the very flow of time that will inevitably cure all ills. Actually time is neutral. It can be used either destructively or constructively. I am coming to feel that the people of ill will have used time much more effectively than the people of good will. We will have to repent in this generation not merely for the vitriolic words and actions of the bad people, but for the appalling silence of the good people. We must come to see that human progress never rolls in on wheels of inevitability. It comes through the tireless efforts and persistent work of men willing to be co-workers with God, and without this hard work time itself becomes an ally of the forces of social stagnation. We must use time creatively, and forever realize that the time is always ripe to do right. Now is the time to make real the promise of democracy, and transform our pending national elegy into a creative psalm of brotherhood. Now is the time to lift our national policy from the quicksand of racial injustice to the solid rock of human dignity.

You spoke of our activity in Birmingham as extreme. At first I was rather disappointed that fellow clergymen would see my nonviolent efforts as those of the extremist. I started thinking about the fact that I stand in the middle of two opposing forces in the Negro community. One is a force of complacency made up of Negroes who, as a result of long years of oppression, have been so completely drained of self-respect and a sense of "somebodiness" that they have adjusted to segregation, and, of a few Negroes in the middle class who, because of a degree of academic and economic security, and because at points they profit by segregation, have unconsciously become insensitive to the problems of the masses. The other force is one of bitterness and hatred, and comes perilously close to advocating violence. It is expressed in the various black nationalist groups that are springing up over the nation, the largest and best known being Elijah Muhammad's Muslim movement. This movement is nourished by the contemporary frustration over the continued existence of racial discrimination. It is made up of people who have lost faith in America, who have absolutely repudiated Christianity, and who have concluded that the white man is an incurable "devil." I have tried to stand between these two forces, saying that we need not follow the "do-nothingism" of the complacent or the hatred and despair of the black nationalist. There is the more excellent way of love and nonviolent protest. I'm grateful to God that, through the Negro church, the dimension of nonviolence entered our struggle. If this philosophy had not emerged, I am convinced that by now many streets of the South would be flowing with floods of blood. And I am further convinced that if our white brothers dismiss us as "rabble-rousers" and "outside agitators" those of us who are working through the channels of nonviolent direct action and refuse to support our nonviolent efforts, millions of Negroes, out of frustration and despair, will seek solace and security in black nationalist ideologies, a development that will lead inevitably to a frightening racial nightmare.

Oppressed people cannot remain oppressed forever. The urge for freedom will eventually come. This is what happened to the American Negro. Something within has reminded him of his birthright of freedom; something without has reminded him that he can gain it. Consciously and unconsciously, he has been swept in by what the Germans call the *Zeitgeist*, and with his black brothers of Africa, and his brown and yellow brothers of Asia, South America and the Caribbean, he is moving with a sense of cosmic urgency toward the promised land of racial justice. Recognizing this vital urge that has engulfed the Negro community, one should readily understand public demonstrations. The Negro has many pent-up resentments and latent frustrations. He has to get them out. .So let him march sometime; let him have his prayer pilgrimages to the city hall; understand why he must have sit-ins and freedom rides. If his repressed emotions do not come out in these nonviolent ways, they will come out in ominous expressions of violence. This is not a threat; it is a fact of history. So I have not said to my people "get rid of your discontent." But I have tried to say that this normal and healthy discontent can be channelized through the creative outlet of nonviolent direct action. Now this approach is being dismissed as extremist. I must admit that I was initially disappointed in being so categorized.

But as I continued to think about the matter I gradually gained a bit of satisfaction from being considered an extremist. Was not Jesus an extremist in love—"Love your enemies, bless them that curse you, pray for them that despitefully use you." Was not Amos an extremist for justice—"Let justice roll down like waters and righteousness like a mighty stream." Was not Paul an extremist for the gospel of Jesus Christ—"I bear in my body the marks of the Lord Jesus." Was not Martin Luther an extremist—"Here I stand; I can do none other so help me God." Was not John Bunyan an extremist—"I will stay in jail to the end of my days before I make a butchery of my conscience." Was not Abraham Lincoln an extremist—"This nation cannot survive half slave and half free." Was not Thomas Jefferson an extremist—"We hold these truths to be self-evident, that all men are created equal." So the question is not whether we will be extremist but what kind of extremist will we be. Will we be extremists for hate or will we be extremists for love? Will we be extremists for the preservation of injustice—or will we be extremists for the cause of justice? In that dramatic scene on Calvary's hill, three men were crucified. We must not forget that all three were crucified for the same crime—the crime of extremism. Two were extremists for immorality, and thusly fell below their environment. The other, Jesus Christ, was an extremist for love, truth and goodness, and thereby rose above his environment. So, after all, maybe the South, the nation and the world are in dire need of creative extremists.

I had hoped that the white moderate would see this. Maybe I was too optimistic. Maybe I expected too much. I guess I should have realized that few members of a race that has oppressed another race can understand or appreciate the deep groans and passionate yearnings of those that have been oppressed and still fewer have the vision to see that injustice must be rooted out by strong, persistent and determined action. I am thankful, however, that some of our white brothers have grasped the meaning of this social revolution and committed themselves to it. They are still all too small in quantity, but they are big in quality. Some like Ralph McGill, Lillian Smith, Harry Golden and James Dabbs have written about our struggle in eloquent, prophetic and understanding terms. Others have marched with us down nameless streets of the South. They have languished in filthy roach-infested jails, suffering the abuse and brutality of angry policemen who see them as "dirty nigger-lovers." They, unlike so many of their moderate brothers and sisters, have recognized the urgency of the moment and sensed the need for powerful "action" antidotes to combat the disease of segregation.

Let me rush on to mention my other disappointment. I have been so greatly disappointed with the white church and its leadership. Of course, there are some notable exceptions. I am not unmindful of the fact that each of you has taken some significant stands on this issue. I commend you, Rev. Stallings, for your Christian stance on this past Sunday, in welcoming Negroes to your worship service on a non-segregated basis. I commend the Catholic leaders of this state for integrating Springhill College several years ago.

But despite these notable exceptions I must honestly reiterate that I have been disappointed with the church. I do not say that as one of the negative critics who can always find something wrong with the church. I say it as a minister of the gospel, who loves the church; who was nurtured in its bosom; who has been sustained by its spiritual blessings and who will remain true to it as long as the cord of life shall lengthen.

I had the strange feeling when I was suddenly catapulted into the leadership of the bus protest in Montgomery several years ago that we would have the support of the white church. I felt that the white ministers, priests and rabbis of the South would be some of our strongest allies. Instead, some have been outright opponents, refusing to understand the freedom movement and misrepresenting its leaders; all too many others have been more cautious than courageous and have remained silent behind the anesthetizing security of the stained glass windows.

In spite of my shattered dreams of the past, I came to Birmingham with the hope that the white religious leadership of this community would see the justice of our cause, and with deep moral concern, serve as the channel through which our just grievances would get to the power structure. I had hoped that each of you would understand. But again I have been disappointed. I have heard numerous religious leaders of the South call upon their worshippers to comply with a desegregation decision because it is the *law*, but I have longed to hear white ministers say, "Follow this decree because integration is morally *right* and the Negro is your brother." In the midst of blatant injustices inflicted upon the Negro, I have watched white churches stand on the sideline and merely mouth pious irrelevancies and sanctimonious trivialities. In the midst of a mighty struggle to rid our nation of racial and economic injustice, I have heard so many ministers say, "Those are social issues with which the gospel has no real concern," and I have watched so many churches commit themselves to a completely otherworldly religion which made a strange distinction between body and soul, the sacred and the secular.

So here we are moving toward the exit of the twentieth century with a religious community largely adjusted to the status quo, standing as a taillight behind other community agencies rather than a headlight leading men to higher levels of justice.

I have traveled the length and breadth of Alabama, Mississippi and all the other southern states. On sweltering summer days and crisp autumn mornings I have looked at her beautiful churches with their lofty spires pointing heavenward. I have beheld the impressive outlay of her massive religious education buildings. Over and over again I have found myself asking: "What kind of people worship here? Who is their God? Where were their voices when the lips of Governor Barnett dripped with words of interposition and nullification? Where were they when Governor Wallace gave the clarion call for defiance and hatred? Where were their voices of support when tired, bruised and weary Negro men and women decided to rise from the dark dungeons of complacency to the bright hills of creative protest?"

Yes, these questions are still in my mind. In deep disappointment, I have wept over the laxity of the church. But be assured that my tears have been tears of love. There can be no deep disappointment where there is not deep love. Yes, I love the church; I love her sacred walls. How could I do otherwise? I am in the rather unique position of being the son, the grandson and the great-grandson of preachers. Yes, I see the church as the body of Christ. But, oh! How we have blemished and scarred that body through social neglect and fear of being nonconformists.

There was a time when the church was very powerful. It was during that period when the early Christians rejoiced when they were deemed worthy to suffer for what they believed. In those days the church was not merely a thermometer that recorded the ideas and principles of popular opinion; it was a thermostat that transformed the mores of society. Wherever the early Christians entered a town the power structure got disturbed and immediately sought to convict them for being "disturbers of the peace" and "outside agitators." But they went on with the conviction that they were "a colony of heaven," and had to obey God rather than man. They were small in number but big in commitment. They were too God-intoxicated to be "astronomically intimidated." They brought an end to such ancient evils as infanticide and gladiatorial contest.

Things are different now. The contemporary church is often a weak, ineffectual voice with an uncertain sound. It is so often the arch-supporter of the status quo. Far from being disturbed by the presence of the church, the power structure of the average community is consoled by the church's silent and often vocal sanction of things as they are.

But the judgement of God is upon the church as never before. If the church of today does not recapture the sacrificial spirit of the early church, it will lose its authentic ring, forfeit the loyalty of millions, and be dismissed as an irrelevant social club with no meaning for the twentieth century. I am meeting young people every day whose disappointment with the church has risen to outright disgust.

Maybe again, I have been too optimistic. Is organized religion too inextricably bound to the status quo to save our nation and the world? Maybe I must turn my faith to the inner spiritual church, the church within the church, as the true *ecclesia* and the hope of the world. But again I am thankful to God that some noble souls from the ranks of organized religion have broken loose from the paralyzing chains of conformity and joined us as active partners in the struggle for freedom. They have left their secure congregations and walked the streets of Albany, Georgia, with us. They have gone through the highways of the South on tortuous rides for freedom. Yes, they have gone to jail with us. Some have been kicked out of their churches, and lost support of their bishops and fellow ministers. But they have gone with the faith that right defeated is stronger than evil triumphant. These men have been the leaven in the lump of the race. Their witness has been the spiritual salt that has preserved the true meaning of the gospel in these troubled times. They have carved a tunnel of hope through the dark mountain of disappointment.

I hope the church as a whole will meet the challenge of this decisive hour. But even if the church does not come to the aid of justice, I have no despair about the future. I have no fear about the outcome of our struggle in Birmingham, even if our motives are presently misunderstood. We will reach the goal of freedom in Birmingham and all over the nation, because the goal of America is freedom. Abused and scorned though we may be, our destiny is tied up with the destiny of America. Before the pilgrims landed at Plymouth we were here. Before the pen of Jefferson etched across the pages of history the majestic words of the Declaration of Independence, we were here. For more than two centuries our foreparents labored in this country without wages; they made cotton king; and they built the homes of their masters in the midst of brutal injustice and shameful humiliation—and yet out of a bottomless vitality they continued to thrive and develop. If the inexpressible cruelties of slavery could not stop us, the opposition we now face will surely fail. We will win our freedom because the sacred heritage of our nation and the eternal will of God are embodied in our echoing demands.

I must close now. But before closing I am impelled to mention one other point in your statement that troubled me profoundly. You warmly commended the Birmingham police force for keeping "order" and "preventing violence." I don't believe you would have so warmly commended the police force if you had seen its angry violent dogs literally biting six unarmed, nonviolent Negroes. I don't believe you would so quickly commend the policemen if you would observe their ugly and inhuman treatment of Negroes here in the city jail; if you would watch them push and curse old Negro women and young Negro girls; if you would see them slap and kick old Negro men and young boys; if you will observe them, as they did on two occasions, refuse to give us food because we wanted to sing our grace together. I'm sorry that I can't join you in your praise for the police department.

It is true that they have been rather disciplined in their public handling of the demonstrators. In this sense they have been rather publicly "nonviolent." But for what purpose? To preserve the evil system of segregation. Over the last few years I have consistently preached that nonviolence demands that the means we use must be as pure as the ends we seek. So I have tried to make it clear that it is wrong to use immoral means to attain moral ends. But now I must affirm that it is just as wrong, or even more so, to use moral means to preserve immoral ends. Maybe Mr. Connor and his policemen have been rather publicly nonviolent, as Chief Pritchett was in Albany, Georgia, but they have used the moral means of nonviolence to maintain the immoral end of flagrant racial injustice. T. S. Eliot has said that there is no greater treason than to do the right deed for the wrong reason.

I wish you had commended the Negro sit-inners and demonstrators of Birmingham for their sublime courage, their willingness to suffer and their amazing discipline in the midst of the most inhuman provocation. One day the South will recognize its real heroes. They will be the James Merediths, courageously and with a majestic sense of purpose facing jeering and hostile mobs and the agonizing loneliness that characterizes the life of the pioneer. They will be old, oppressed, battered Negro women, symbolized in a seventy-two-year-old woman of Montgomery, Alabama, who rose up with a sense of dignity and with her people decided not to ride the segregated buses, and responded to one who inquired about her tiredness with ungrammatical profundity: "My feet is tired, but my soul is rested." They will be the young high school and college students, young ministers of the gospel and a host of their elders courageously and nonviolently sitting-in at lunch counters and willingly going to jail for conscience's sake. One day the South will know that when these disinherited children of God sat down at lunch counters they were in reality standing up for the best in the American dream and the most sacred values in our Judeo-Christian heritage, and thusly, carrying our whole nation back to those great wells of democracy which were dug deep by the Founding Fathers in the formulation of the Constitution and the Declaration of Independence.

Never before have I written a letter this long (or should I say book?). I'm afraid that it is much too long to take your precious time. I can assure you that it would have been much shorter if I had been writing from a comfortable desk, but what else is there to do when you are alone for days in the dull monotony of a narrow jail cell other than write long letters, think strange thoughts, and pray long prayers?

If I have said anything in this letter that is an overstatement of the truth and is indicative of an unreasonable impatience, I beg you to forgive me. If I have said anything in this letter that is an understatement of the truth and is indicative of my having a patience that makes me patient with anything less than brotherhood, I beg God to forgive me.

I hope this letter finds you strong in the faith. I also hope that circumstances will soon make it possible for me to meet each of you, not as an integrationist or a civil rights leader, but as a fellow clergyman and a Christian brother. Let us all hope that the dark clouds of racial prejudice will soon pass away and the deep fog of misunderstanding will be lifted from our fear-drenched communities and in some not too distant tomorrow the radiant stars of love and brotherhood will shine over our great nation with all of their scintillating beauty.

Yours for the cause of Peace and Brotherhood,

Martin Luther King, Jr.

Martin Luther King, Jr., Why We Can't Wait (New York: Harper & Row, 1963, 1964). The American Friends Committee first published this essay as a pamphlet. It has probably been reprinted more than anything else Dr. King wrote.

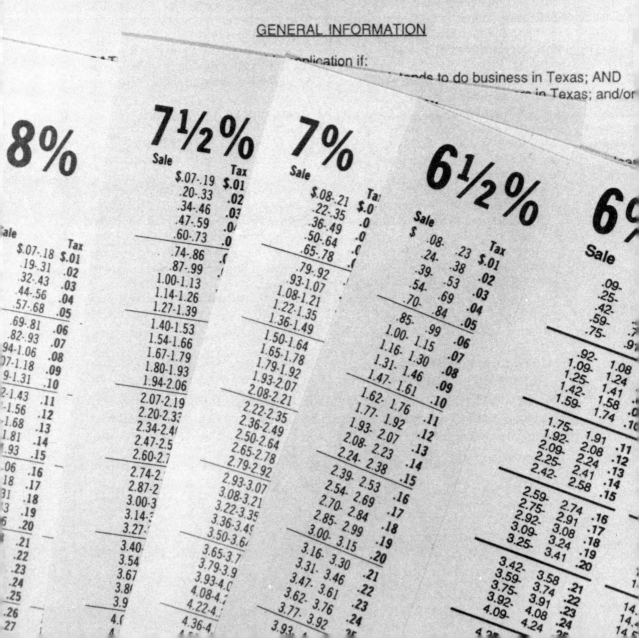

Lesson 26

Fiscal Policy in Texas

Overview

Education, highways, human services, law enforcement, and prisons are examples of services provided by the state of Texas. But government services must be paid for. The average Texan pays more than $1500 in state and local taxes. A substantial sum? Of course, but, by national standards, it is below average. Texas ranks in the bottom third of states in the amount of its state and local taxes.

The size of the Texas budget has increased each biennium. And we can be sure that, in this growing state with myriad needs, the budget will continue to increase. As the population of the state increases, it takes more money to pay for law enforcement, prisons, education, and highways.

Inflation and demand for new services fuel the increase in the cost of state government. In recent years, even more money has been needed, because Texas has been under court orders to improve the quality of education, care in schools for the mentally retarded, and prisons. To put additional money into mental health care, education, and prisons requires either reducing expenditures in other programs or raising additional revenues. Since Texas provides only minimum funds for most programs, cuts in these programs are not really feasible. So meeting these court orders requires the expenditure of even more money and raising even more revenue.

The political process by which decisions are made about how money will be allocated and how funds are raised is called fiscal policy. Fiscal policy is more than a boring technical process of budget estimates of revenue and spending, appropriations bills, and finance bills. It is a process in which decisions affect the lives of each Texan: How much will we pay in sales tax? What will the quality of public education be in Texas? How much money must be raised on the local level through additional property taxes? Will critically ill children receive life-saving medical care? How good do we want our roads and highways to be? How large should the Texas prison system be? Will we have clean air and water?

These decisions are political decisions made first by our elected officials. Reaching agreement on such decisions often involves compromise, trade-offs, and *quid pro quo* deals – and this can be an exciting process. Certainly, it is a process which each Texan should follow, because it directly affects our own wallet. Each of us consents to the decisions by our vote; those who do not vote, acquiesce to the decisions of others through their own apathy.

Learning Objectives

Goal: The purpose of this lesson is to describe Texas' fiscal policy and budgetary process and to examine changes necessary for Texas to meet continuing revenue needs.

Objectives:

1. Explain reasons why declining revenues and demands for increased services caused financial crisis in Texas during the 1980s.

2. Describe policies of fiscal management that have guided Texas government, using opinions from Ann Richards and assigned readings.

3. Identify sources of revenue, both current and proposed, for securing funds for state government in Texas.
   List four major categories of spending by state government in Texas, including value received from expenditures and causes for increases in budgets.

5. Discuss the impact of high technology and biotechnology on the financial future of the state of Texas.

Key Terms

Watch for these terms and pay particular attention to what each one means, as you follow the textbook and telelesson.

Fiscal year	Selective sales tax
Fiscal policy	Severance tax
Regressive tax	Bond
Progressive tax	High technology (TV)
General sales tax	Biotechnology (TV)

Textbook Reading Assignment

Jones, Ericson, Brown, and Trotter. *Practicing Texas Politics,* 8th edition. Chapter 9, "Revenues, Expenditures, and Fiscal Policy," pp. 421-476.

Jones, Ericson, Brown, Trotter, and Lynch. *Practicing Texas Politics – A Brief Survey,* 4th. edition. Chapter 9, "Revenues, Expenditures, and Fiscal Policy," pp. 262-294.

Note to student: You are responsible for only *one* of these reading assignments. It is your responsibility to know which book is used in your class.

Textbook Focus Points

Before you read the textbook assignment, review the following points to help focus your thoughts. After you complete the assignment, write your responses to reinforce what you have learned.

1. Why were there fiscal crises in 1984 and 1986? Describe demands for increased spending for education, welfare, water, state employees' salaries, Texas' highway system, and prison reform. Why did the state lack funds?

2. What are Texas' traditional fiscal policies and policies of budgeting and fiscal management? How have Texas' budget, taxing, and spending policies affected overall fiscal policy?

3. How does Texas obtain its revenues? Describe the general sales tax, selective sales taxes, "sin taxes," and severance taxes. What are the major non-tax sources of revenue for Texas?

4. What are the procedures for Texas incurring bonded indebtedness?

5. What are the four major categories of spending for the State of Texas? Evaluate whether Texas receives a dollar in value for each dollar spent.

6. How will Texas raise additional revenues for budget increases?

7. Describe the readings "How Your Tax Dollars Are Spent" (Jones, 8th ed. and Survey, 4th ed.), "Speaking His Mind on Taxes and Texas Finance" (Jones, 8th ed.), and "New Tax Helping Stamp Out Drugs" (Survey, 4th ed.).

Telelesson Interviewees

The following individuals will share their expertise in the telelesson:

Kevin Blackistone–Financial Columnist, *Dallas Morning News*
Kent Caperton–Member, Texas Senate, Bryan
Charldean Newell–Department of Political Science, University of North Texas
Ann Richards–Governor and former State Treasurer
Bernard Winestein–Director, Institute for Economic Development, University of North Texas
Mary Young–Department of Political Economy, University of Texas at Dallas

Telelesson Focus Points

Before viewing the telelesson, read the following points to help focus your thoughts. After the presentation, write your responses to help you remember these important points.

1. According to Bernard Winestein, what is high technology and biotechnology?

2. What caused the major financial crises of the 1980s in Texas? What should be done to prevent future financial crises?

3. What causes increases in the state budget?

4. According to Ann Richards, what is the objective of state deposits and investments?

5. What will be the major sources of revenue for Texas in the future? What is the likelihood of Texas enacting a personal or corporate income tax? Do state income taxes deter business?

Recommended Reading

The following suggestions are not required unless your instructor assigns them. They are listed to let you know where you can find additional information on areas which interest you.

Bennett, Scott. "Getting Rid of the Abacus." *Texas Business* (September 1983): pp. 51-53.

Eckhardt, Bob. "Time to Tax Corporate Income." *Texas Observer* (March 20, 1987): pp. 8-9.

Fiscal Notes. Office of the Comptroller (Monthly): Austin, Texas 78711.

Holley, Joe. "Hobby, Bullock Call the Shots." *Texas Observer* (April 8, 1983): pp. 5-7.

Lipari, Lisbeth. "Income Texas." *Texas Observer* (July 12, 1991): pp. 4-5,15. Proposals for personal and corporate income taxes.

Getting Involved

This activity is not required unless your instructor assigns it. But it offers good suggestions to help you understand and become more involved in the political process.

Read articles which address the issue of corporate and personal income taxes for Texas, especially those that consider the enactment of an income tax and reduction in sales and property taxes. Consider the effect of an income tax on your personal life. Write a brief paper in which you explain whether the enactment of an income tax and the reduction of other taxes would result in you paying more or less in state and local taxes.

Self Test

After reading the assignment and watching the telelesson, you should be able to answer these questions. When you have completed the test, turn to the Answer Key to score your answers.

1. Texas' fiscal crises in the 1980s were **most** directly related to
   a. levels of agricultural production.
   b. booms and busts in high technology industries.
   c. oil prices.
   d. variations in federal grant-in-aid programs.

2. In the midst of the state's economic transition and nationwide inflation, citizen groups in Texas increased their demands for
   a. more state spending for both education and highways.
   b. more state spending for education but less state spending for highways.
   c. less state spending for education but more state spending for highways.
   d. less state spending for both education and highways.

---

3. The Texas Constitution specifies that the state budget must cover
   a. one year.
   b. one or two years.
   c. two years.
   d. a period of time authorized by the legislature and approved by the governor.

4. Every two years budgets are submitted to the Texas legislature by the Legislative Budget Board and the
   a. Judicial Budget Office.
   b. Executive Budget Office.
   c. Administrative Budget Office.
   d. Comptroller's Office.

5. The basic function of the state auditor is to provide the legislature with a check on the integrity and efficiency of the
   a. counties.
   b. legislative branch.
   c. judicial branch.
   d. executive branch.

6. For Texas state government, the most important single source of tax revenue is the tax on
   a. personal income.
   b. sales.
   c. real estate.
   d. services.

7. A payroll tax is levied for the purpose of insuring workers against
   a. illness.
   b. unemployment.
   c. injury on the job.
   d. old age.

8. After the record-setting tax increase in 1987 and other increases since then, Texans are paying _____ tax burden placed on other states' residents.
   a. well below the average
   b. the average
   c. well above the average
   d. four times the average

9. Any bond or other obligation issued by or on behalf of the State of Texas must be approved by the
   a. comptroller of public accounts and the state auditor.
   b. governor and secretary of state.
   c. Legislative Budget Board.
   d. Bond Review Board.

10. The most expensive public service of Texas' budget is
   a. highways and public transportation.
   b. correctional facilities.
   c. education.
   d. health and human services.

11. Revenue from Permanent University Fund investments is shared by
   a. four-year universities outside the University of Texas and Texas A&M University systems.
   b. privately endowed professional schools in Texas.
   c. all public universities in Texas.
   d. the University of Texas and Texas A&M University systems.

12. Texas' spending for transportation encourages motor vehicle use to the detriment of other forms of transportation, especially
   a. mass transit systems.
   b. bicycle riding in urban areas.
   c. hiking in rural areas.
   d. using boats and barges on rivers and canals.

13. You are a resident of the State of Texas, and last year you paid $895 in taxes to the state. According to Joe Ericson, in "How Your Texas Tax Dollars Are Spent," what is the single largest state expenditure of your tax dollars?
    a. Matching funds that allow Texas to qualify for federal aid.
    b. Colleges and universities in the state.
    c. Human service programs such as welfare.
    d. Elementary and high school education.

14. According to Bernard Winestein, high technology is
    a. not an important part of the Texas economy.
    b. concentrated in the Rio Grande Valley.
    c. a method of enhancing productivity in the workplace.
    d. seldom used in Texas manufacturing and industry.

15. Improvements in the making of wine or cheese and raising livestock is
    a. biotechnology.
    b. physical science.
    c. computer technology.
    d. pharmaceutical technology.

16. Fiscal crises of the 1980s were caused, in large part, by
    a. declining population.
    b. refusal of major corporations to pay the state franchise fee.
    c. decline in oil prices.
    d. over-valuation of the Mexican peso.

17. In Texas, increases in the state's budget can be accounted for by population growth, inflation, and
    a. court orders to improve public services.
    b. bureaucratic inefficiencies.
    c. governmental waste.
    d. mandates of regional accrediting associations.

18. According to Ann Richards, primary objectives for depositing state funds in banks and other investment decisions are safety and
    a. private support for governmental programs.
    b. producing revenue that reduces the need for taxes.
    c. participation in Texas elections.
    d. prompt handling of state accounts.

19. In Texas, a major source of revenue for the state will continue to be
    a. vehicle registration fees.
    b. franchise fees.
    c. sales taxes.
    d. amusement machine taxes.

20. According to experts, a corporate and individual income tax
    a. will never be enacted in Texas.
    b. is prohibited by the Texas Constitution.
    c. will not be enacted in Texas for twenty more years.
    d. is inevitable.

21. According to Mary Young, a corporate and individual income tax in Texas would
    a. not deter business in Texas.
    b. be less fair than the present corporate franchise tax.
    c. be supported by a majority of the legislature.
    d. be unacceptable to most Texans.

Answer Key

These are the correct answers with reference to the Learning Objectives, and to the source of the information: the Textbook Focus Points, Jones, *et al. Practicing Texas Politics* (Jones) or Jones, *et. al., Practicing Texas Politics — A Brief Survey* (Survey); the Study Guide Overview (Overview); and the Telelesson Focus Points. Page numbers are also given for the Textbook Focus Points. "KT" indicates questions with Key Terms defined.

Question	Answer	Learning Objective	Textbook Focus Point (page no.)	Telelesson Focus Point
1	C	1	1 (Jones, pp. 422-423; Survey, pp. 263-264)	
2	A	1	1 (Jones, p. 423; Survey, p. 264)	
3	C	2	2 (Jones, p. 426; Survey, pp. 266-267)	
4	B	2	2 (Jones, pp. 427-428; Survey, p. 268)	
5	D	2	2 (Jones, p. 433; Survey, pp. 271-272)	
6	B	3	3 (Jones, pp. 434-435; Survey, pp. 273-274)	
7	B	3	3 (Jones, p. 439; Survey, p. 275)	
8	A	3	3 (Jones, p. 441; Survey, p. 276)	
9	D	3	4 (Jones, p. 446; Survey, p. 279)	
10	C	4	5 (Jones, pp. 448-449; Survey, pp. 280-281)	
11	D	4	5 (Jones, p. 453; Survey, p. 284)	
12	A	4	5 (Jones, pp. 456-457; Survey, p. 286)	
13	D	4	7 (Jones, pp. 475-476; Survey, pp. 293-294)	
14	C	5		1
15	A	5		1
16	C	1		2
17	A	4		3
18	B	2		4
19	C	3		5
20	D	3		5
21	A	3		5